The Oxford Poetry Library

GENERAL EDITOR: FRANK KERMODE

ANDREW MARVELL (1621–78) lived through some of the most momentous events in English history, but his poetry is detached and private, mostly lyrical, strikingly original in its combining of existing traditions, and seemingly untouched for the most part by what was happening around him. He left Cambridge on the death of his father and travelled on the Continent, possibly to avoid direct involvement in the civil wars. Later, back in England, he worked (like his friend John Milton) for the government of Oliver Cromwell, and still later, after the Restoration of Charles II, he strove in opposition as MP for Hull. This last period led to more direct involvement in political affairs. Most of his poems were published after his death in a volume (1681) edited by a woman claiming to be his widow. For a century and more after his death he was remembered primarily as a witty satirist in verse and a polemicist in prose.

FRANK KERMODE, retired King Edward VII Professor of English Literature at Cambridge, the General Editor of the Oxford Poetry Library, and co-editor of this particular volume, is the author of many books, including *Romantic Image*, *The Sense of an Ending*, *The Classic*, *The Genesis of Secrecy*, *Forms of Attention*, and *History and Value*.

KEITH WALKER is Senior Lecturer in English Language and Literature at University College London. He has written on eighteenth-century literature, and edited a selection of the works of Dryden for the Oxford Poetry Library.

THE OXFORD POETRY LIBRARY

GENERAL EDITOR: FRANK KERMODE

Matthew Arnold	*Miriam Allott*
William Blake	*Michael Mason*
Byron	*Jerome McGann*
Samuel Taylor Coleridge	*Heather Jackson*
John Dryden	*Keith Walker*
Thomas Hardy	*Samuel Hynes*
George Herbert	*Louis Martz*
Gerald Manley Hopkins	*Catherine Phillips*
Ben Jonson	*Ian Donaldson*
John Keats	*Elizabeth Cook*
Andrew Marvell	*Frank Kermode and Keith Walker*
John Milton	*Jonathan Goldberg and Stephen Orgel*
Alexander Pope	*Pat Rogers*
Sir Philip Sidney	*Katherine Duncan-Jones*
Henry Vaughan	*Louis Martz*
William Wordsworth	*Stephen Gill and Duncan Wu*

The Oxford Poetry Library

Andrew Marvell

Edited by
FRANK KERMODE
and
KEITH WALKER

Oxford   New York
OXFORD UNIVERSITY PRESS
1994

Oxford University Press, Walton Street, Oxford OX2 6DP

Oxford New York Toronto
Delhi Bombay Calcutta Madras Karachi
Kuala Lumpur Singapore Hong Kong Tokyo
Nairobi Dar es Salaam Cape Town
Melbourne Auckland Madrid
and associated companies in
Berlin Ibadan

Oxford is a trade mark of Oxford University Press

British Library Cataloguing in Publication Data
Data available

Library of Congress Cataloging in Publication Data
Marvell, Andrew, 1621–1678
[Poems. Selections]
Andrew Marvell / edited by Frank Kermode and Keith Walker.
p. cm. — (The Oxford poetry library)
Includes bibliographical references.
I. Kermode, Frank, 1919– . II. Walker, Keith, 1936– .
III. Title. IV. Series.
821'.4—dc20 PR3546.A6 1994 93–34646
ISBN 0-19-282271-3

1 3 5 7 9 10 8 6 4 2

Typeset by J&L Composition Ltd.
Printed in Great Britain by Biddles Ltd,
Guildford and King's Lynn

Contents

Introduction

When Marvell died in 1678, the government was considering an informer's report which named him as the author of *An Account of the Growth of Popery*. The report was correct, and the informer said nothing that was not widely known. At the time of the poet's death all the talk must have been of this and similar works which attacked the deviousness of the king, and his failure to prevent his brother from plotting a French papist takeover in England. Marvell was the satirist, the controversialist, expert in the joint territories of politics and religion; he was the classical republican, sketching in advance the principles of 1688, and an eighteenth-century man before his time. His epitaph in St Giles, London, grants him 'wit and learning, with a singular penetration and strength of judgment', but whereas we should use these words of the poet, the writer of the tribute thought of him exclusively as a patriot politician. When his *Miscellaneous Poems* appeared in 1681, they were read in dissenting circles but otherwise attracted little attention, though his satirical fame was great, and people thought him the author of a considerable body of anti-Establishment writing with which he had had nothing to do.

The consequences of having been born in 1621 were in some way like those of having been born in 1918: the course of a man's life must have been strongly affected by war and the aftermath of war. So, after 1642, it was with Marvell. There was nothing very unusual about his youth. Though of Cambridgeshire stock, he was born in Yorkshire, where his father was a parson of strong Calvinist convictions. Given this background it is not surprising that the poet went—at the age of 12—from Hull Grammar School to Cambridge. Some said that as a student he was tempted by the Jesuits, but rescued from them by his father. When his father drowned in the Humber in 1641 Marvell left Trinity College and went to London. After that, as we know from Milton's letter recommending him to the President of the Council of State in 1653, Marvell travelled for some four years in Europe, possibly to avoid the Civil War, possibly as a tutor to some young gentleman, possibly even as some kind of government agent, and certainly to use his chance to learn languages such as Spanish, Italian, French and Dutch—all of which would prove useful in a diplomatic or political, as well as in a literary, career. He was certainly in Rome in 1645 or 1646, when he wrote the satirical verses about Richard Flecknoe (see p. 75); in December 1645 he met Lord Francis Villiers there.

Before his travels, Marvell had written a Latin and Greek poem addressed to the King in a Cambridge collection of 1637 (Marvell's first Horatian Ode). He must have been back in London by 1648, when he wrote the elegy for Lord Francis Villiers, killed in the second Civil War in July of that year (see p. 1).

Of Marvell's politics at this time little positive can be said; though Villiers was certainly a royalist, as was Lovelace, in whose book Marvell in 1649 published commendatory verses. Lord Hastings, for whom he wrote an elegy in the same year, was also royalist.

In 1650, a year of change both political and personal, Marvell went to Yorkshire and became tutor to Mary, daughter of the Parliamentary general Lord Fairfax, with whom he had a remote family connection. He remained there for more than two years. Fairfax, though in a position of great authority, had unsuccessfully opposed the execution of the king in 1649, and in 1650 the invasion of Scotland, which was undertaken in his place by Cromwell, fresh from his expedition to 'pacify' Ireland.

At this point Marvell, though not actively involved, could hardly avoid at least a contemplation of politics. The peculiar interest of Fairfax's position was that he had voluntarily and on principle withdrawn from eminence and settled into a studious country retirement. It is obvious from 'Upon Appleton House' that Marvell greatly admired Fairfax. Perhaps, as is sometimes suggested by critics examining the nuances of 'Upon Appleton House', he had mixed feelings about his employer's choice of life, though sympathizing with the motives for it. Later he was to say that men ought to have trusted the king, yet without making it plain at this stage that he was now, with whatever reservations, on the side of the new regime. The reason why there is so much uncertainty about his position is that at this period he expressed himself not in prose but in poetry, with a higher degree of obliquity and a concern for more than topical significance. 'An Horatian Ode on Cromwell's Return from Ireland' is a manifestly great poem, yet it is also baffling to anybody who wants simply to know where the poet stood with Cromwell in 1650. There has been a great deal of interpretation, some of it of high quality, but the poem remains resistant to decoding.

The palpable complexity of its political references is in itself a deterrent to over-simplification, and there are also certain rather intractable difficulties of a bibliographical kind. The Ode is, ostensibly, a poem of the sort that celebrates the arrival or departure of some great person on a notable occasion, the great man on this occasion being Cromwell. Yet at the very centre of the poem is a long and apparently sympathetic account of a different and even more solemn occasion—not the return of Cromwell, but the final departure of the king. There is an ambiguity of tone not unlike that of Horace's great Actium Ode (i.37), in which a somewhat brazen celebration of Octavian's victory modulates into a splendid, and as it were reluctant, tribute to the defeated Cleopatra.

The occasion dates the poem, which must have been written between Cromwell's return from Ireland in May 1650 and his preventive campaign against Scotland, begun in June 1650. The poet was at Nun Appleton, presumably in close contact with Fairfax and doubtless thinking hard about the great issues. Of course he had not been obliged, as Fairfax had, to make firm decisions and act on them, and it would be unsafe to assume that he fully shared his employer's disapproval of the Scottish campaign, or indeed of the regicide. That event he placed at the centre of the Ode, in an obvious tribute to its absolute importance; it is the point at which the horizontal and the vertical of history could be thought to cross. The echoes of Horace and Lucan reinforce this sense of historical crisis; Lucan is concerned with the crisis caused by Julius Caesar's violation of the ancient rights, his casting of the ancient republic into another mould, and his assumption of the role of dictator or protector. Horace celebrates Actium, the battle which assured the forced imperial power of Augustus. Charles was an English king and in terms of imperialist history not only the inheritor of Lucan's crisis but the negative image of Horace's—the ruin of the great work of time, not its beginnings.

The complexity of the entire poem—characteristic of the complexity of all Marvell's best poetry—can perhaps be briefly illustrated by a consideration of the central passage on the death of the king. It ostensibly develops the point about Cromwell's 'wiser art', his reputed skill in ensuring the capture of the king by the Parliament. Now the king is produced on a scaffold, such as might be used by strolling players, but fixed outside the Banqueting House built by the king's father for the masquing in which Charles had often taken part. Now he must perform the death of a great man, himself; he is an actor, and this is his last act. His performance on this 'scene' is admirable, and the verse enacts it in a soft cadence:

> Nor called the gods with vulgar spite
> To vindicate his helpless right,
>> But bowed his comely head
>> Down as upon a bed . . .

But this quiet solemnity is merely a preparation for the startling drum-roll of the next lines:

> This was that memorable hour
> Which first assured the forced power—

followed by the triumphal metaphor of the bleeding head, and the celebration of Cromwell's ruthless achievements as the servant of the new republic—a soldier who knows that rights hold or break not in so far as they are ancient, but as men are strong or weak; a man who hardly needs to have it explained that 'the same arts that did gain | A power must it maintain'.

The poem, whether by allusion or by significant silences, is extremely topical. As Michael Wilding among others has pointed out,[1] Cromwell was by this time rather more than an obedient servant of Parliament; if the poem hints at this it does no more than hint. Some think Marvell is endorsing a Machiavellian dictator, while others argue that his rhetorical tone is one of admiring caution. A Machiavellian (and Marvell had been called that) would say that in the real world what men do is more important than what they ought to do; things as they are and not as we would have them. Perhaps the profession of admiration for the king, and the deliberate, concessive tone of some of the praise of Cromwell ('And if we would speak true, | Much to the man is due') are merely rhetorical feints, and Marvell really was, with only a few reservations, committed to the new order, to the crossing of this Rubicon. The means might appear wicked, but God sometimes works by such means, as when Samson married Delilah so as, in the process of a divine plot, to pull down the pillars on the Philistian nobles.

But the poem as a whole seems resistant to simple and even to sophisticated explanations, whether political or rhetorical. Perhaps

---

[1] Michael Wilding, 'Marvell's "An Horation Ode upon Cromwell's Return from Ireland", the Levellers, and the Junta', *Dragons Teeth: Literature of the English Revolution* (Oxford, 1987) 114–137.

it has always been so. Its first success seems to have been with royalists, but it was excluded from *1681* (though two extant copies include it) presumably because it was read, in the light of the poet's subsequent career, as being clearly on Cromwell's side. And despite the vast quantity of modern exegesis a certain obscurity remains. It is deepened by our failure fully to explain the relation between the Ode and the poem 'Tom May's Death', which speaks of 'ancient rights' and does not disparage them (see the notes on that poem, p. 155).

The chronology of Marvell's poems is far from certain, except of course when their occasion is obvious, as with 'An Horatian Ode' and such works as 'The Character of Holland' and the poem on the first anniversary of Cromwell's protectorate. It would be difficult to deny that it was during his Nun Appleton period that Marvell wrote the Bilbrough and Appleton House poems, and it is usually assumed, though there is no direct evidence, that in those years he also wrote 'The Garden' and the series of Mower poems. These are distinctive not only because mowers were unusual pastoral subjects, being considered lower than shepherds (a point contested by Marvell's mower), but also because there are so many differences between the poems themselves. All, however, are beautifully fashioned, and all extend the scope of the genres and sub-genres to which they can be assigned. They are works of extraordinary refinement, with the long tradition of ancient and Renaissance pastoral behind them, yet here transfigured. And it is true that Marvell's poems, even when they most resemble those of other poets, or are most in the fashions of time, usually have a quite distinctive tone.

In 1653 he became tutor to William Dutton, a ward of Cromwell's, and lived at Eton in the house of John Oxenbridge, whose knowledge of the Bermudas probably contributed to Marvell's poem on the subject. Now close to Cromwell, he wrote songs for the marriage of Cromwell's daughter Mary in 1657. In the same year he was appointed Latin Secretary to the Council of State, the post for which the blind Milton, now needing such assistance, had unsuccessfully recommended him four years earlier. (He may have repaid that debt by playing a part in saving Milton's life after the Restoration.) Together with Milton and Dryden, he walked in Cromwell's funeral procession in 1658 and wrote a poem on the Protector's death, which among other things pledged support to Richard Cromwell, the son who briefly succeeded Oliver in that quasi-regal office. In 1659 Marvell became Member of Parliament for Hull.

When Richard was dislodged and Parliament dissolved there followed a period of political confusion, but Marvell again represented Hull in the Convention Parliament of 1660, which recalled Charles II. Any difficulty his adherence to Cromwell may have caused him was ended by an Act of Oblivion of 1660, which excepted only a dozen names, Marvell's not being among them. Charles managed without elections, and Marvell continued to represent Hull with admirable assiduity, as his correspondence demonstrates, until his death, though for a time he quarrelled with the other Hull member, Colonel Gilby. John Kenyon remarks that Marvell was leading a double life, as a pedestrian MP and 'a prominent though usually anonymous opposition spokesman', as in his 'Last Instructions to a Painter'.[2] He was habitually and savagely critical of the Court.

In the early 1660s Marvell went to Holland on an uknown mission and accompanied the Earl of Carlisle on a lengthy embassy to Russia, Sweden, and Denmark. In his remaining years he was primarily a politician, devotedly anti-Catholic and pro-Nonconformist, though the exact nature of his own religion is characteristically ambiguous and obscure. It was as defender of liberty against foreign and domestic threats—some of which took the form of religion—and as the advocate of a monarchical state less absolute than the Stuarts had always wanted that he was remembered in the following century, and indeed in Wordsworth's time, though it was in that time also that poets began to look with interest at his lyric poetry.

Marvell's prose work *The Rehearsal Transprosed* of 1672, and its second part (1673)—which, unlike the first, was published under his name—were called by Gilbert Burnet 'the wittiest books that have appeared in this age'. His target was Samuel Parker, a successful parson, later a bishop, who had written in favour of legally enforced religious conformity. Affirming the country's need for more rather than less tolerance, Marvell in a famous passage looked back upon the Civil War. It was no longer worth asking whether it had been fought for religion or liberty; indeed, he said, 'I think the Cause was too good to have been fought for. Men ought to have trusted God; they ought and might have trusted the King

---

[2] 'Andrew Marvell: Life and Times', in R.L. Brett (ed.), *Andrew Marvell* (Oxford, 1979), 1–35.

with the whole matter.' It seems unlikely that he had felt the same way in 1650. Now, many years later, he appears to be saying that both sides had been wrong, that the king, being still the centre and source of power, ought himself to have prevented the conflict.

The interest of the remainder of Marvell's life is largely political. He was probably under government surveillance, for he was strong in opposition, and even invited, or stumbled into, a brawl with the Speaker of the House, who censured him for his unparliamentary conduct. In 1677 he wrote, anonymously, *An Account of the Growth of Popery and Arbitrary Government*, against the supposed plot of English Catholics, abetted by Louis XIV, to catholicize England—incidentally taking every chance of attacking ministerial and parliamentary corruption. (This was the year before the Popish Plot). He seems to have had a hot temper, yet he was on occasion devious and often wrote anonymously. As remarked earlier, the government offered a reward for information about the authorship of *The Growth of Popery* and had in their hands an informer's report naming Marvell when he died in 1678 (poisoned—it was rumoured —by the Jesuits). He died suddenly after a trip to Hull, and was doubtless immersed in these and other dangerous troubles.

There is some mystery about the publication in 1681 of the *Miscellaneous Poems* 'by Andrew Marvell, Esq; late Member of the Honourable House of Commons'. The book is prefaced by a Note to the Reader: 'These are to certify every ingenious reader, that all these poems, as also the other things in this book contained, are printed according to the exact copies of my late dear husband, under his own hand-writing, being found since his death among his other papers, witness my hand this 15th day of October, 1680.' Despite the energetic advocacy of the late Sir William Empson, Mary Palmer's claim to have been married to Marvell is not generally believed. The poet was associated with a business founded in 1671 by Richard Thompson, a cousin, and Edward Nelthorpe, a more remote kinsman. Another cousin, Edward Thompson, was also involved. The firm was bankrupted in 1676, having lost, according to some accounts, the very large sum of £60,000. Marvell took lodgings in Great Russell Street for his associates to hide from the creditors. But he and Nelthorpe died within a month of each other, and the fiction, if such it was, that Mary Palmer was Marvell's wife seems to have been part of a trick to ensure that a bond of £500 entered into by the poet should not be forfeited to the creditors. Marvell's estate was apparently extremely small, and

£500 would be useful. Mary Palmer's deposition maintained that Marvell had made her promise not to reveal their marriage, and she complied by behaving more like a servant than a wife. Empson's long, lively, detailed, and quixotic essay is an attempt to confute the standard account. He believed Mary was speaking the truth: the marriage, though clandestine and probably performed at a church specializing in such unions, was nevertheless valid, its object being, as in all such cases, 'to delay the announcement, not to hide the truth for ever.' However, the volume of the relevant church register needed to prove this theory is missing. Empson further speculates that Marvell was homosexual and that he must have been relieved to discover, somewhat belatedly, that he enjoyed sex with a woman.[3] However that may be, Thomas Cooke, who had talked to the poet's nieces, affirmed in the short biography included in his 1726 edition that Marvell 'never married', and Tupper's evidence, though damaged a little by Empson's genial ferocity, seems strong enough to confirm that view.

It would seem then that the ambiguities, the uncommittedness, of the poems reflected some of the same qualities in Marvell's life. John Aubrey described him as 'of middling stature, pretty strong set, roundish faced, cherry cheeked, hazel eye ... he was in his conversation very modest, and of very few words; Though he loved wine he would never drink hard in company; and was wont to say, "that he would not play the good-fellow in any man's company in whose hands he would not trust his life."' Aubrey also suggests that Marvell used drink as a stimulus to poetry. He sounds like a man often morose and always private. He had friends, including Harrington and Milton,[4] and he had a family and business associates; but on the whole we may think of him as a reserved, passionate man. Some of his political poetry deserves to be called odious, and no doubt there were equally reprehensible passages in his political dealings generally; but on the whole the respect in which he came to be held as a defender of liberty and rational government was justified.

Although a handful of his lyrics was republished in Tonson's various miscellanies early in the eighteenth century, only the satires

---

[3] 'The Marriage of Marvell', *Using Biography* (1984), 43–95. The standard view is based on F.S. Tupper, 'Mary Palmer, *alias* Mrs Andrew Marvell', *PMLA*, 53 (1938), 367–92.

[4] Christopher Hill, 'Milton and Marvell', in C.A. Patrides (ed.), *Approaches to Marvell* (1978), 1–30.

achieved immediate posthumous celebrity. The two eighteenth-century editions were largely undertaken to ensure the survival of his reputation as a patriot. It was in the nineteenth century, in America as well as in England, that the emphasis altered, but full acceptance of the 'metaphysical' poetry came when the prejudice against 'conceited' or 'metaphysical' poetry was overthrown in the twentieth century. The foundation of much modern criticism is T.S. Eliot's tercentenary essay of 1921, still in many respects the finest single essay on Marvell. The first Oxford edition, Margoliouth's followed in 1927 (2nd edn. 1952; 3rd edn. revised by Pierre Legouis and Elsie Duncan-Jones, 1971) and Pierre Legouis's vast doctoral study, *André Marvell: Poète, Puritain, Patriote*, in 1928 (there is a shorter version in English, published in 1965). The last two decades have seen many additions to the understanding of Marvell's politics as well as to that of his poetry, not least in the numerous and various contributions of E.E. Duncan-Jones, now the doyenne of Marvell scholarship. Some modern studies are included in our select list of Further Reading (p. 170): to have admitted more would have defeated our purpose, for the volume of criticism and scholarship on Marvell is now bewildering and continues to grow. It seems there is always something more to be said of Marvell.

Chronology

Note on the Text

This edition contains those English poems in *Miscellaneous Poems* (1681), which we are reasonably sure are by Marvell, and a few poems separately published. The texts of the poems are modernized versions of those given in H.M. Margoliouth's standard Oxford edition (3rd edn., revised by Pierre Legouis with the collaboration of E.E. Duncan-Jones, 1971), though the originals have also been consulted.

An Elegy upon the Death of my Lord Francis Villiers

'Tis true that he is dead: but yet to choose,
Methinks thou, Fame, should not have brought the news;
Thou canst discourse at will and speak at large:
But wast not in the fight nor durst thou charge;
While he transported all with valiant rage
His name eternized, but cut short his age;
On the safe battlements of Richmond's bowers
Thou wast espied, and from the gilded towers
Thy silver trumpets sounded a retreat
Far from the dust and battle's sulphury heat.   10
Yet what couldst thou have done? 'Tis always late
To struggle with inevitable fate.
Much rather thou, I know, expect'st to tell
How heavy Cromwell gnashed the earth and fell.
Or how slow death far from the sight of day
The long-deceived Fairfax bore away.
But until then, let us young Francis praise:
And plant upon his hearse the bloody bays,
Which we will water with our welling eyes.
Tears spring not still from spungy cowardice.   20
The purer fountains from the rocks more steep
Distil and stony valour best doth weep.
Besides revenge, if often quenched in tears,
Hardens like steel and daily keener wears.
  Great Buckingham, whose death doth freshly strike
Our memories, because to this so like.
Ere that in the eternal court he shone,
And here a favourite, there found a throne,
The fatal night before he hence did bleed,
Left to his princess this immortal seed,   30
As the wise Chinese in the fertile womb
Of earth doth a more precious clay entomb,
Which dying, by his will he leaves consigned:
Till by mature delay of time refined
The crystal metal fit to be released
Is taken forth to crown each royal feast:
Such was the fate by which this posthume breathed,
Who scarcely seems begotten but bequeathed.
  Never was any human plant that grew
More fair than this and acceptably new.   40

'Tis truth that beauty doth most men dispraise:
Prudence and valour their esteem do raise.
But he that hath already these in store,
Can not be poorer sure for having more.
And his unimitable handsomeness
Made him indeed be more than man, not less.
We do but faintly God's resemblance bear
And like rough coins of careless mints appear:
But he of purpose made, did represent
In a rich medal every lineament.   50
    Lovely and admirable as he was,
Yet was his sword or armour all his glass.
Nor in his mistress' eyes that joy he took,
As in an enemy's himself to look.
I know how well he did, with what delight
Those serious imitations of fight.
Still in the trials of strong exercise
His was the first, and his the second prize.
    Bright lady, thou that rulest from above
The last and greatest monarch of love: 60
Fair Richmond, hold thy brother or he goes.
Try if the jasmine of they hand or rose
Of thy red lip can keep him always here.
For he loves danger and doth never fear.
Or may thy tears prevail with him to stay?
    But he, resolved, breaks carelessly away.
Only one argument could now prolong
His stay and that most fair and so most strong:
The matchless Clora whose pure fires did warm
His soul and only could his passions charm.   70
    You might with much more reason go reprove
The amorous magnet which the north doth love.
Or preach divorce, and say it is amiss
That with tall elms the twining vines should kiss,
Than chide two such so fit, so equal fair
That in the world they have no other pair,
Whom it might seem that heaven did create
To restore man unto his first estate.
Yet she for honour's tyrannous respect
Her own desires did, and his neglect.   80
And like the modest plant at every touch
Shrunk in her leaves and feared it was too much.

But who can paint the torments and that pain
Which he professed and now she could not feign?
He like the sun but overcast and pale:
She like a rainbow, that ere long must fail,
Whose roseal cheek where heaven itself did view
Begins to separate and dissolve to dew.
    At last he leave obtains though sad and slow,
First of her and then of himself to go.   90
How comely and how terrible he sits
At once, and war as well as love befits!
Ride where thou wilt and bold adventures find:
But all the ladies are got up behind.
Guard them, though not thyself: for in they death
The eleven thousand virgins lose their breath.
    So Hector issuing from the Trojan wall
The sad Iliads to the gods did call,
With hands displayed and with dishevelled hair,
That they the empire in his life would spare,   100
While he secure through all the field doth spy
Achilles, for Achilles only cry.
Ah, ignorant that yet ere night he must
Be drawn by him inglorious through the dust.
    Such fell young Villiers in the cheerful heat
Of youth: his locks entangled all with sweat
And those eyes which the sentinel did keep
Of love, closed up in an eternal sleep.
While Venus of Adonis thinks no more
Slain by the harsh tusk of the savage boar.   110
Hither she runs and hath him buried far
Out of the noise and blood, and killing war:
Where in her gardens of sweet myrtle laid
She kisses him in the immortal shade.
    Yet died he not revengeless: much he did
Ere he could suffer. A whole pyramid
Of vulgar bodies he erected high:
Scorning without a sepulchre to die.
And with his steel which did whole troops divide
He cut his epitaph on either side.   120
Till finding nothing to his courage fit
He rid up last to death and conquered it.
    Such are the obsequies to Francis own:
He best the pomp of his own death hath shown.

And we hereafter to his honour will
Not write so many, but so many kill.
Till the whole army by just vengeance come
To be at once his trophy and his tomb.

To his Noble Friend Mr Richard Lovelace, upon his Poems

Sir,
Our times are much degenerate from those
Which your sweet muse with your fair fortune chose,
And as complexions alter with the climes,
Our wits have drawn the infection of our times.
That candid age no other way could tell
To be ingenious, but by speaking well.
Who best could praise had then the greatest praise,
'Twas more esteemed to give than wear the bays:
Modest ambition studied only then
To honour not herself but worthy men.   10
These virtues now are banished out of town,
Our Civil Wars have lost the civic crown.
He highest builds, who with most art destroys,
And against others' fame his own employs.
I see the envious caterpillar sit
On the fair blossom of each growing wit.
   The air's already tainted with the swarms
Of insects which against you rise in arms:
Word-peckers, paper-rats, book-scorpions,
Of wit corrupted, the unfashioned sons.   20
The barbed censurers begin to look
Like the grim consistory on thy book;
And on each line cast a reforming eye,
Severer than the young presbytery.
Till when in vain they have thee all perused,
You shall, for being faultless, be accused.
Some reading your *Lucasta* will allege
You wronged in her the House's privilege.
Some that you under sequestration are,
Because you writ when going to the war,   30
And one the book prohibits, because Kent
Their first petition by the author sent.

But when the beauteous ladies came to know
That their dear Lovelace was endangered so:
Lovelace that thawed the most congealed breast—
He who loved best and them defended best,
Whose hand so rudely grasps the steely brand,
Whose hand so gently melts the lady's hand—
They all in mutiny though yet undressed
Sallied, and would in his defence contest.   40
And one, the loveliest that was yet e'er seen,
Thinking that I too of the rout had been,
Mine eyes invaded with a female spite,
(She knew what pain 'twould be to lose that sight.)
'O no, mistake not,' I replied, 'for I
In your defence, or in his cause, would die.'
But he, secure of glory and of time,
Above their envy, or mine aid, doth climb.
Him valiant'st men and fairest nymphs approve;
His book in them finds judgement, with you love.   50

Upon the death of Lord Hastings

Go, intercept some fountain in the vein,
Whose virgin-source yet never steeped the plain.
Hastings is dead, and we must find a store
Of tears untouched, and never wept before.
Go, stand betwixt the morning and the flowers;
And, ere they fall, arrest the early showers.
Hastings is dead; and we, disconsolate,
With early tears must mourn his early fate.
  Alas, his virtues did his death presage:
Needs must he die, that doth out-run his age.   10
The phlegmatic and slow prolongs his day,
And on time's wheel sticks like a remora.
What man is he that hath not heaven beguiled,
And is not thence mistaken for a child?
While those of growth more sudden, and more bold,
Are hurried hence, as if already old.
For, there above, they number not as here,
But weigh to man the geometric year.
  Had he but at this measure still increased,
And on the Tree of Life once made a feast,   20

As that of Knowledge; what loves had he given
To earth, and then what jealousies to heaven!
But 'tis a maxim of the state, that none,
Lest he become like them, taste more than one.
Therefore the democratic stars did rise,
And all that worth from hence did ostracize.

Yet as some prince, that, for state-jealousy,
Secures his nearest and most loved ally;
His thought with richest triumphs entertains,
And in the choicest pleasures charms his pains: 30
So he, not banished hence, but there confined,
There better recreates his active mind.

Before the crystal palace where he dwells,
The armed angels hold their carousels;
And underneath, he views the tournaments
Of all these sublunary elements.
But most he doth the eternal book behold,
On which the happy names do stand enrolled;
And gladly there can all his kindred claim,
But most rejoices at his mother's name.   40

The gods themselves cannot their joy conceal,
But draw their veils, and their pure beams reveal:
Only they drooping Hymeneus note,
Who, for sad purple, tears his saffron coat;
And trails his torches through the starry hall
Reversed at his darling's funeral.
And Aesculapius, who, ashamed and stern,
Himself at once condemneth, and Mayern
Like some sad chemist, who, prepared to reap
The golden harvest, sees his glasses leap.   50
For, how immortal must their race have stood,
Had Mayern once been mixed with Hastings' blood!
How sweet and verdant would these laurels be,
Had they been planted on that balsam tree!

But what could he, good man, although he bruised
All herbs, and them a thousand ways infused?
All he had tried, but all in vain, he saw,
And wept, as we, without redress or law.
For man (alas) is but the heaven's sport;
And art indeed is long, but life is short.   60

A Dialogue, between the Resolved Soul and
Created Pleasure

Courage, my soul, now learn to wield
The weight of thine immortal shield.
Close on thy head thy helmet bright.
Balance thy sword against the fight.
See where an army, strong as fair,
With silken banners spreads the air.
Now, if thou be'st that thing divine,
In this day's combat let it shine:
And show that Nature wants an art
To conquer one resolved heart.   10

PLEASURE

Welcome the creation's guest,
Lord of earth, and heaven's heir.
Lay aside that warlike crest,
And of Nature's banquet share:
Where the souls of fruits and flowers
Stand prepared to heighten yours.

SOUL

I sup above, and cannot stay
To bait so long upon the way.

PLEASURE

On these downy pillows lie,
Whose soft plumes will thither fly: 20
On these roses strewed so plain
Lest one leaf thy side should strain

SOUL

My gentler rest is on a thought,
Conscious of doing what I ought.

PLEASURE

If thou be'st with perfumes pleased,
Such as oft the gods appeased,
Thou in fragrant clouds shalt show
Like another god below.

SOUL

A soul that knows not to presume
Is heaven's and its own perfume.   30

PLEASURE

Everything does seem to vie
Which should first attract thine eye:
But since none deserves that grace,
In this crystal view *thy* face.

SOUL

When the creator's skill is prized,
The rest is all but earth disguised.

PLEASURE

Hark how music then prepares
For thy stay these charming airs;
Which the posting winds recall,
And suspend the river's fall.   40

SOUL

Had I but any time to lose,
On this I would it all dispose.
Cease, tempter. None can chain a mind
Whom this sweet chordage cannot bind.

CHORUS

Earth cannot show so brave a sight
As when a single soul does fence
The batteries of alluring sense,
And heaven views it with delight.
   Then persevere: for still new charges sound:
   And if thou overcom'st, thou shalt be crowned.   50

PLEASURE

All this fair, and soft, and sweet,
   Which scatteringly doth shine,
Shall within one beauty meet,
   And she be only thine.

SOUL

If things of sight such heavens be,
What heavens are those we cannot see?

PLEASURE

Wheresoe'er thy foot shall go
   The minted gold shall lie,
Till thou purchase all below,
   And want new world to buy.   60

SOUL

Were't not a price, who'd value gold?
And that's worth naught that can be sold.

PLEASURE

Wilt thou all the glory have
   That war or peace commend?
Half the world shall be thy slave
   The other half thy friend.

SOUL

What friends, if to my self untrue!
What slaves, unless I captive you!

PLEASURE

Thou shalt know each hidden cause;
   And see the future time: 70
Try what depth the centre draws;
   And then to heaven climb.

SOUL

None thither mounts by the degree
Of knowledge, but humility.

CHORUS

Triumph, triumph, victorious soul;
The world has not one pleasure more:
The rest does lie beyond the pole,
And is thine everlasting store.

On a Drop of Dew

See how the orient dew,
Shed from the bosom of the morn
　　Into the blowing roses,
Yet careless of its mansion new;
For the clear region where 'twas born
　　Round in itself encloses:
　　And in its little globe's extent,
Frames as it can its native element.
　　How it the purple flower does slight,
　　　Scarce touching where it lies,   10
　　But gazing back upon the skies,
　　　Shines with a mournful light,
　　　　Like its own tear,
Because so long divided from the sphere.
　　Restless it rolls and unsecure,
　　　Trembling lest it grow impure,
　　Till the warm sun pity its pain,
And to the skies exhale it back again.
　　So the soul, that drop, that ray
Of the clear fountain of eternal day,   20
Could it within the human flower be seen,
　　Remembering still its former height,
　　Shuns the swart leaves and blossoms green,
　　And recollecting its own light,
Does, in its pure and circling thoughts, express
The greater heaven in a heaven less.
　　In how coy a figure wound,
　　Every way it turns away:
　　So the world excluding round,
　　Yet receiving in the day,   30
　　Dark beneath, but bright above,

Here disdaining, there in love.
How loose and easy hence to go,
How girt and ready to ascend,
Moving but on a point below,
It all about does upwards bend.
Such did the manna's sacred dew distil,
White and entire, though congealed and chill,
Congealed on earth: but does, dissolving, run
Into the glories of the almighty sun.   40

The Coronet

When for the thorns with which I long, too long,
    With many a piercing wound,
    My saviour's head have crowned,
I seek with garlands to redress that wrong:
    Through every garden, every mead,
I gather flowers (my fruits are only flowers),
    Dismantling all the fragrant towers
That once adorned my shepherdess's head.
And now when I have summed up all my store,
    Thinking (so I myself deceive)   10
    So rich a chaplet thence to weave
As never yet the king of glory wore:
    Alas, I find the serpent old
    That, twining in his speckled breast,
    About the flowers disguised does fold,
    With wreaths of fame and interest.
Ah, foolish man, that wouldst debase with them,
And mortal glory, heaven's diadem!
But thou who only couldst the serpent tame,
Either his slippery knots at once untie;   20
And disentangle all his winding snare;
Or shatter too with him my curious frame,
And let these wither, so that he may die,
Though set with skill and chosen out with care:
That they, while thou on both their spoils dost tread,
May crown thy feet, that could not crown thy head.

Eyes and Tears

1

How wisely Nature did decree,
With the same eyes to weep and see!
That, having viewed the object vain,
They might be ready to complain.

2

And since the self-deluding sight,
In a false angle takes each height,
These tears, which better measure all,
Like watery lines and plummets fall.

3

Two tears, which Sorrow long did weigh
Within the scales of either eye,   10
And then paid out in equal poise,
Are the true price of all my joys.

4

What in the world most fair appears,
Yea, even laughter, turns to tears:
And all the jewels which we prize,
Melt in these pendants of the eyes.

5

I have through every garden been,
Amongst the red, the white, the green,
And yet, from all the flowers I saw,
No honey but these tears, could draw.   20

6

So the all-seeing sun each day
Distils the world with chemic ray,
But finds the essence only showers
Which straight in pity back he pours.

7

Yet happy they whom grief doth bless,
That weep the more, and see the less:
And, to preserve their sight more true,
Bathe still their eyes in their own dew.

8

So Magdalen, in tears more wise
Dissolved those captivating eyes,   30
Whose liquid chains could flowing meet
To fetter her Redeemer's feet.

9

Not full sails hasting loaden home,
Nor the chaste lady's pregnant womb,
Nor Cynthia teeming shows so fair,
As two eyes swollen with weeping are.

10

The sparkling glance that shoots desire,
Drenched in these waves does lose its fire.
Yea, oft the thunderer pity takes
And here the hissing lightning slakes.   40

11

The incense was to heaven dear,
Not as a perfume, but a tear.
And stars show lovely in the night,
But as they seem the tears of light.

12

Ope then, mine eyes, your double sluice,
And practise so your noblest use;
For others too can see, or sleep,
But only human eyes can weep.

13

Now, like two clouds dissolving, drop,
And at each tear in distance stop: 50
Now, like two fountains, trickle down;
Now, like two floods o'erturn and drown.

14

Thus let your streams o'erflow your springs,
Till eyes and tears be the same things:
And each the other's difference bears;
These weeping eyes, those seeing tears.

Bermudas

Where the remote Bermudas ride
In the ocean's bosom unespied,
From a small boat, that rowed along,
The listening winds received this song.
  'What should we do but sing his praise
That led us through the watery maze,
Unto an isle so long unknown,
And yet far kinder than our own?
Where he the huge sea-monsters wracks,
That lift the deep upon their backs,   10
He lands us on a grassy stage,
Safe from the storms, and prelate's rage.
He gave us this eternal spring,
Which here enamels everything,
And sends the fowls to us in care,
On daily visits through the air.
He hangs in shades the orange bright,
Like golden lamps in a green night,
And does in the pom'granates close
Jewels more rich than Ormus shows.   20
He makes the figs our mouths to meet,
And throws the melons at our feet,
But apples plants of such a price,
No tree could ever bear them twice.
With cedars, chosen by his hand,
From Lebanon, he stores the land,
And makes the hollow seas, that roar,
Proclaim the ambergris on shore.
He cast (of which we rather boast)
The gospel's pearl upon our coast,   30
And in these rocks for us did frame

A temple, where to sound his name.
Oh let our voice his praise exalt,
Till it arrive at heaven's vault;
Which thence (perhaps) rebounding, may
Echo beyond the Mexique Bay.'
Thus sung they, in the English boat,
A holy and a cheerful note,
And all the way, to guide their chime,
With falling oars they kept the time.   40

Clorinda and Damon

C. Damon, come drive thy flocks this way.
D. No, 'tis too late; they went astray.
C. I have a grassy scutcheon spied,
   Where Flora blazons all her pride.
   The grass I aim to feast thy sheep:
   The flowers I for thy temples keep.
D. Grass withers; and the flowers too fade.
C. Seize the short joys then, ere they vade.
   Seest thou that unfrequented cave?
D. That den?   10
C.   Love's shrine.
D.   But virtue's grave.
C. In whose cool bosom we may lie
   Safe from the sun.
D.   Not heaven's eye.
C. Near this, a fountain's liquid bell
   Tinkles within the concave shell.
D. Might a soul bathe there and be clean,
   Or slake its drought?
C.   What is't you mean?
D. These once had been enticing things,
   Clorinda, pastures, caves, and springs.
C. And what late change?
D.   The other day
   Pan met me.
C.   What did great Pan say?   20
D. Words that transcend poor shepherds' skill,

But he e'er since my songs does fill:
And his name swells my slender oat.
C. Sweet must Pan sound in Damon's note.
D. Clorinda's voice might make it sweet.
C. Who would not in Pan's praises meet?

CHORUS
Of Pan the flowery pastures sing,
Caves echo, and the fountains ring.
Sing then while he doth us inspire;
For all the world is our Pan's choir.   30

A Dialogue between the Soul and Body

SOUL
O, who shall from this dungeon raise
A soul, enslaved so many ways,
With bolts of bones, that fettered stands
In feet, and manacled in hands.
Here blinded with an eye; and there
Deaf with the drumming of an ear.
A soul hung up, as 'twere, in chains
Of nerves, and arteries, and veins.
Tortured, besides each other part,
In a vain head, and double heart?   10

BODY
O, who shall me deliver whole,
From bonds of this tyrannic soul?
Which, stretched upright, impales me so,
That mine own precipice I go;
And warms and moves this needless frame
(A fever could but do the same),
And, wanting where its spite to try,
Has made me live to let me die.
A body that could never rest,
Since this ill spirit is possessed.   20

SOUL

What magic could me thus confine
Within another's grief to pine,
Where, whatsoever it complain,
I feel, that cannot feel, the pain.
And all my care itself employs,
That to preserve, which me destroys:
Constrained not only to endure
Diseases, but, what's worse, the cure:
And ready oft the port to gain,
And shipwrecked into health again?   30

BODY

But physic yet could never reach
The maladies thou me dost teach:
Whom first the cramp of hope does tear,
And then the palsy shakes of fear;
The pestilence of love does heat,
Or hatred's hidden ulcer eat;
Joy's cheerful madness does perplex,
Or sorrow's other madness vex;
Which knowledge forces me to know,
And memory will not forgo.   40
What but a soul could have the wit
To build me up for sin so fit?
So architects do square and hew,
Green trees that in the forest grew.

The Nymph complaining for the
Death of her Fawn

The wanton troopers riding by
Have shot my fawn, and it will die.
Ungentle men! They cannot thrive
To kill thee. Thou ne'er didst alive
Them any harm: alas, nor could
Thy death yet do them any good.
I'm sure I never wished them ill;
Nor do I for all this; nor will:

But if my simple prayers may yet
Prevail with heaven to forget   10
Thy murder, I will join my tears
Rather than fail. But, O my fears!
It cannot die so. Heaven's King
Keeps register of everything:
And nothing may we use in vain.
E'en beasts must be with justice slain,
Else men are made their deodands.
Though they should wash their guilty hands
In this warm life-blood, which doth part
From thine, and wound me to the heart,   20
Yet could they not be clean: their stain
Is dyed in such a purple grain,
There is not such another in
The world, to offer for their sin.

Unconstant Sylvio, when yet
I had not found him counterfeit,
One morning (I remember well),
Tied in this silver chain and bell,
Gave it to me: nay, and I know
What he said then; I'm sure I do.   30
Said he, 'Look how your huntsman here
Hath taught a fawn to hunt his *dear*.'
But Sylvio soon had me beguiled.
This waxed tame, while he grew wild,
And quite regardless of my smart,
Left me his fawn, but took his heart.

Thenceforth I set myself to play
My solitary time away
With this: and very well content,
Could so mine idle life have spent.   40
For it was full of sport; and light
Of foot, and heart; and did invite
Me to its game; it seemed to bless
Itself in me. How could I less
Than love it? O I cannot be
Unkind, t'a beast that loveth me.

Had it lived long, I do not know
Whether it too might have done so
As Sylvio did: his gifts might be

Perhaps as false or more than he.   50
But I am sure, for ought that I
Could in so short a time espy,
Thy love was far more better than
The love of false and cruel men.
　　With sweetest milk, and sugar, first
I it at mine own fingers nursed.
And as it grew, so every day
It waxed more white and sweet than they.
It had so sweet a breath! And oft
I blushed to see its foot more soft,   60
And white (shall I say than my hand?)
Nay, any lady's of the land.
　　It is a wondrous thing, how fleet
'Twas on those little silver feet.
With what a pretty skipping grace,
It oft would challenge me the race:
And when't had left me far away,
'Twould stay, and run again, and stay.
For it was nimbler much than hinds;
And trod, as on the four winds.   70
　　I have a garden of my own
But so with roses overgrown,
And lilies, that you would it guess
To be a little wilderness.
And all the springtime of the year
It only loved to be there.
Among the beds of lilies, I
Have sought it oft, where it should lie;
Yet could not, till itself would rise,
Find it, although before mine eyes.   80
For, in the flaxen lilies' shade,
It like a bank of lilies laid.
Upon the roses it would feed,
Until its lips e'en seemed to bleed:
And then to me 'twould boldly trip,
And print those roses on my lip.
But all its chief delight was still
On roses thus itself to fill:
And its pure virgin limbs to fold
In whitest sheets of lilies cold.   90

Had it lived long, it would have been
Lilies without, roses within.
   O help! O help! I see it faint:
And die as calmly as a saint.
See how it weeps. The tears do come
Sad, slowly dropping like a gum.
So weeps the wounded balsam: so
The holy frankincense doth flow.
The brotherless Heliades
Melt in such amber tears as these.   100
   I in a golden vial will
Keep these two crystal tears; and fill
It till it do o'erflow with mine;
Then place it in Diana's shrine.
   Now my sweet fawn is vanished to
Whither the swans and turtles go:
In fair Elysium to endure,
With milk-white lambs, and ermines pure.
O do not run too fast: for I
Will but bespeak thy grave, and die.   110
   First my unhappy statue shall
Be cut in marble; and withal,
Let it be weeping too—but there
The engraver sure his art may spare,
For I so truly thee bemoan,
That I shall weep though I be stone:
Until my tears, still dropping, wear
My breast, themselves engraving there.
There at my feet shalt thou be laid,
Of purest alabaster made: 120
For I would have thine image be
White as I can, though not as thee.

Young Love

I

Come, little infant, love me now,
   While thine unsuspected years
Clear thine aged father's brow
   From cold jealousy and fears.

2

Pretty, surely, 'twere to see
  By young love old time beguiled,
While our sportings are as free
  As the nurse's with the child.

3

Common beauties stay fifteen;
  Such as yours should swifter move,   10
Whose fair blossoms are too green
  Yet for lust, but not for love.

4

Love as much the snowy lamb,
  Or the wanton kid, does prize,
As the lusty bull or ram,
  For his morning sacrifice.

5

Now then love me: time may take
  Thee before thy time away:
Of this need we'll virtue make,
  And learn love before we may.   20

6

So we win of doubtful fate;
  And if good she to us meant,
We that good shall antedate,
  Or, if ill, that ill prevent.

7

Thus as kingdoms, frustrating
  Other titles to their crown,
In the cradle crown their king,
  So all foreign claims to drown,

8

So, to make all rivals vain,
  Now I crown thee with my love: 30
Crown me with thy love again,
  And we both shall monarchs prove.

To his coy Mistress

Had we but world enough, and time,
This coyness, lady, were no crime.
We would sit down, and think which way
To walk, and pass our long love's day.
Thou by the Indian Ganges' side
Shouldst rubies find: I by the tide
Of Humber would complain. I would
Love you ten years before the flood:
And you should, if you please, refuse
Till the conversion of the Jews.   10
My vegetable love should grow
Vaster than empires, and more slow.
A hundred years should go to praise
Thine eyes, and on thy forehead gaze.
Two hundred to adore each breast:
But thirty thousand to the rest.
An age at least to every part,
And the last age should show your heart:
For, lady, you deserve this state;
Nor would I love at lower rate.   20
    But at my back I always hear
Time's winged chariot hurrying near:
And yonder all before us lie
Deserts of vast eternity.
Thy beauty shall no more be found;
Nor, in thy marble vault, shall sound
My echoing song: then worms shall try
That long-preserved virginity:
And your quaint honour turn to dust;
And into ashes all my lust.   30
The grave's a fine and private place,
But none, I think, do there embrace.
    Now, therefore, while the youthful hue
Sits on thy skin like morning dew,
And while thy willing soul transpires
At every pore with instant fires,
Now let us sport us while we may;
And now, like amorous birds of prey,

Rather at once our time devour,
Than languish in his slow-chapped power.   40
Let us roll all our strength, and all
Our sweetness, up into one ball:
And tear our pleasures with rough strife,
Thorough the iron gates of life.
Thus, though we cannot make our sun
Stand still, yet we will make him run.

The unfortunate Lover

1

Alas, how pleasant are their days
With whom the infant Love yet plays!
Sorted by pairs, they still are seen
By fountains cool, and shadows green.
But soon these flames do lose their light,
Like meteors of a summer's night:
Nor can they to that region climb,
To make impression upon time.

2

'Twas in a shipwreck, when the seas
Ruled, and the winds did what they please,   10
That my poor lover floating lay,
And, ere brought forth, was cast away:
Till at the last the master-wave
Upon the rock his mother drave;
And there she split against the stone,
In a Caesarean section.

3

The sea him lent these bitter tears
Which at his eyes he always bears:
And from the winds the sighs he bore,
Which through his surging breast do roar.   20
No day he saw but that which breaks
Through frighted clouds in forked streaks,
While round the rattling thunder hurled,
As at the funeral of the world.

4

While Nature to his birth presents
This masque of quarrelling elements,
A numerous fleet of cormorants black,
That sailed insulting o'er the wrack,
Received into their cruel care
Th'unfortunate and abject heir: 30
Guardians most fit to entertain
The orphan of the hurricane.

5

They fed him up with hopes and air,
Which soon digested to despair,
And as one cormorant fed him, still
Another on his heart did bill.
Thus while they famish him, and feast,
He both consumed, and increased:
And languished with doubtful breath,
The amphibium of life and death.   40

6

And now, when angry heaven would
Behold a spectacle of blood,
Fortune and he are called to play
At sharp before it all the day:
And tyrant Love his breast does ply
With all his winged artillery,
Whilst he, betwixt the flames and waves,
Like Ajax, the mad tempest braves.

7

See how he nak'd and fierce does stand,
Cuffing the thunder with one hand,   50
While with the other he does lock,
And grapple, with the stubborn rock:
From which he with each wave rebounds,
Torn into flames, and ragg'd with wounds,
And all he says, a lover dressed
In his own blood does relish best.

8

This is the only banneret
That ever Love created yet:
Who though, by the malignant stars,
Forced to live in storms and wars;   60
Yet dying leaves a perfume here,
And music within every ear:
And he in story only rules,
In a field sable a lover gules.

The Gallery

1

Clora, come view my soul, and tell
Whether I have contrived it well.
Now all its several lodgings lie
Composed into one gallery;
And the great arras-hangings, made
Of various faces, by are laid;
That, for all furniture, you'll find
Only your picture in my mind.

2

Here thou are painted in the dress
Of an inhuman murderess;   10
Examining upon our hearts
Thy fertile shop of cruel arts:
Engines more keen than ever yet
Adorned tyrant's cabinet;
Of which the most tormenting are
Black eyes, red lips, and curled hair.

3

But, on the other side, th'art drawn
Like to Aurora in the dawn;
When in the East she slumbering lies,
And stretches out her milky thighs;   20
While all the morning choir does sing,

And manna falls, and roses spring;
And, at thy feet, the wooing doves
Sit perfecting their harmless loves.

4

Like an enchantress here thou showst,
Vexing thy restless lover's ghost;
And, by a light obscure, dost rave
Over his entrails, in the cave;
Divining thence, with horrid care,
How long thou shalt continue fair;   30
And (when informed) them throwst away,
To be the greedy vulture's prey.

5

But, against that, thou sitst afloat
Like Venus in her pearly boat.
The halcyons, calming all that's nigh,
Betwixt the air and water fly;
Or, if some rolling wave appears,
A mass of ambergris it bears.
Nor blows more wind that what may well
Convey the perfume to the smell.   40

6

These pictures and a thousand more
Of thee my gallery does store
In all the forms thou canst invent
Either to please me, or torment:
For thou alone to people me,
Art grown a numerous colony;
And a collection choicer far
Than or Whitehall's or Mantua's were.

7

But, of these pictures and the rest,
That at the entrance likes me best: 50
Where the same posture, and the look
Remains, with which I first was took:

A tender shepherdess, whose hair
Hangs loosely playing in the air,
Transplanting flowers from the green hill,
To crown her head, and bosom fill.

The Fair Singer

1

To make a final conquest of all me,
Love did compose so sweet an enemy,
In whom both beauties to my death agree,
Joining themselves in fatal harmony;
That while she with her eyes my heart does bind,
She with her voice might captivate my mind.

2

I could have fled from one but singly fair:
My disentangled soul itself might save,
Breaking the curled trammels of her hair;
But how should I avoid to be her slave,   10
Whose subtle art invisibly can wreathe
My fetters of the very air I breathe?

3

It had been easy fighting in some plain,
Where victory might hang in equal choice.
But all resistance against her is vain,
Who has the advantage both of eyes and voice,
And all my forces needs must be undone,
She having gained both the wind and sun.

Mourning

1

You, that decipher out the fate
Of human offsprings from the skies,
What mean these infants which of late
Spring from the stars of Clora's eyes?

2

Her eyes confused, and doubled o'er,
With tears suspended ere they flow,
Seem bending upwards, to restore
To heaven, whence it came, their woe.

3

When, moulding of the watery spheres,
Slow drops untie themselves away,   10
As if she, with those precious tears,
Would strow the ground where Strephon lay.

4

Yet some affirm, pretending art,
Her eyes have so her bosom drowned,
Only to soften near her heart
A place to fix another wound.

5

And, while vain pomp does her restrain
Within her solitary bower,
She courts herself in amorous rain;
Herself both Danae and the shower.   20

6

Nay, others, bolder, hence esteem
Joy now so much her master grown,
That whatsoever does but seem
Like grief, is from her windows thrown.

7

Nor that she pays, while she survives,
To her dead love this tribute due,
But casts abroad these donatives,
At the installing of a new.

8

How wide they dream! The Indian slaves
That sink for pearl through seas profound   30
Would find her tears yet deeper waves
And not of one the bottom sound.

9

I yet my silent judgement keep,
Disputing not what they believe:
But sure as oft as women weep,
It is to be supposed they grieve.

Daphnis and Chloe

1

Daphnis must from Chloe part:
Now is come the dismal hour
That must all his hopes devour,
All his labour, all his art.

2

Nature, her own sex's foe,
Long had taught her to be coy:
But she neither knew t'enjoy,
Nor yet let her lover go.

3

But with this sad news surprised,
Soon she let that niceness fall,   10
And would gladly yield to all,
So it had his stay comprised.

4

Nature so herself does use
To lay by her wonted state,
Lest the world should separate;
Sudden parting closer glues.

5

He, well-read in all the ways
By which men their siege maintain,
Knew not that the fort to gain,
Better 'twas the siege to raise.   20

6

But he came so full possessed
With the grief of parting thence,
That he had not so much sense
As to see he might be blessed.

7

Till love in her language breathed
Words she never spake before,
But, than legacies no more,
To a dying man bequeathed.

8

For, alas, the time was spent,
Now the latest minute's run   30
When poor Daphnis is undone,
Between joy and sorrow rent.

9

At that 'Why', that 'Stay, my dear',
His disordered locks he tare;
And with rolling eyes did glare,
And his cruel fate forswear.

10

As the soul of one scarce dead,
With the shrieks of friends aghast,
Looks distracted back in haste,
And then straight again is fled;   40

11

So did wretched Daphnis look,
Frighting her he loved most.
At the last, this lover's ghost
Thus his leave resolved took.

12

'Are my hell and heaven joined
More to torture him that dies?
Could departure not suffice,
But that you must then grow kind?

13

'Ah, my Chloe, how have I
Such a wretched minute found,   50
When they favours should me wound
More than all thy cruelty?

14

'So to the condemned wight
The delicious cup we fill;
And allow him all he will,
For his last and short delight.

15

'But I will not now begin
Such a debt unto my foe;
Nor to my departure owe
What my presence could not win.   60

16

'Absence is too much alone:
Better 'tis to go in peace,
Than my losses to increase
By a late fruition.

17

'Why should I enrich my fate?
'Tis a vanity to wear,
For my executioner,
Jewels of so high a rate.

18

'Rather I away will pine
In a manly stubborness   70
Than be fatted up express
For the cannibal to dine.

19

'Whilst this grief does thee disarm,
All th' enjoyment of our love
But the ravishment would prove
Of a body dead while warm.

20

'And I parting should appear
Like the gourmand Hebrew dead,
While with quails and manna fed,
He does through the desert err.   80

21

'Or the witch that midnight wakes
For the fern, whose magic weed
In one minute casts the seed,
And invisible him makes.

22

'Gentler times for love are meant:
Who for parting pleasure strain
Gather roses in the rain,
Wet themselves, and spoil their scent.

23

'Farewell, therefore, all the fruit
Which I could from love receive: 90
Joy will not with sorrow weave,
Nor will I this grief pollute.

24

'Fate, I come, as dark, as sad,
As thy malice could desire;
Yet bring with me all the fire
That Love in his torches had.'

25

At these words away he broke;
As who long has praying lien,
To his headsman makes the sign,
And receives the parting stroke.   100

26

But hence, virgins, all beware:
Last night he with Phlogis slept;
This night for Dorinda kept;
And but rid to take the air.

27

Yet he does himself excuse;
Nor indeed without a cause:
For, according to the laws,
Why did Chloe once refuse?

The Definition of Love

1

My love is of a birth as rare
As 'tis for object strange and high:
It was begotten by Despair
Upon Impossibility.

2

Magnanimous Despair alone
Could show me so divine a thing,
Where feeble Hope could ne'er have flown
But vainly flapped its tinsel wing.

3

And yet I quickly might arrive
Where my extended soul is fixed,   10
But Fate does iron wedges drive,
And always crowds itself betwixt.

4

For Fate with jealous eyes does see
Two perfect loves, nor lets them close:
Their union would her ruin be,
And her tyrannic power depose.

5

And therefore her decrees of steel
Us as the distant Poles have placed,
(Though Love's whole world on us doth wheel)
Not by themselves to be embraced,   20

6

Unless the giddy heaven fall,
And earth some new convulsion tear;
And, us to join, the world should all
Be cramped into a planisphere.

7

As lines (so loves) oblique may well
Themselves in every angle greet:
But ours so truly parallel,
Though infinite, can never meet.

8

Therefore the love which us doth bind,
But Fate so enviously debars,   30
Is the conjunction of the mind,
And opposition of the stars.

The Picture of Little T.C. in a Prospect of Flowers

1

See with what simplicity
This nymph begins her golden days!
In the green grass she loves to lie,
And there with her fair aspect tames
The wilder flowers, and gives them names:
But only with the roses plays;
   And them does tell
What colour best becomes them, and what smell.

2

Who can foretell for what high cause
This darling of the gods was born!   10
Yet this is she whose chaster laws
The wanton Love shall one day fear,
And, under her command severe,
See his bow broke and ensigns torn.
   Happy, who can
Appease this virtuous enemy of man!

3

O, then let me in time compound,
And parley with those conquering eyes;
Ere they have tried their force to wound,
Ere, with their glancing wheels, they drive   20
In triumph over hearts that strive,
And them that yield but more despise.
           Let me be laid,
Where I may see thy glories from some shade.

4

Meantime, whilst every verdant thing
Itself does at thy beauty charm,
Reform the errors of the spring;
Make that the tulips may have share
Of sweetness, seeing they are fair;
And roses of their thorns disarm: 30
           But most procure
That violets may a longer age endure.

5

But, O young beauty of the woods,
Whom Nature courts with fruits and flowers,
Gather the flowers, but spare the buds;
Lest Flora angry at thy crime,
To kill her infants in their prime,
Do quickly make the example yours;
           And, ere we see,
Nip in the blossom all our hopes and thee.

The Match

I

Nature had long a treasure made
  Of all her choicest store;
Fearing, when she should be decayed,
  To beg in vain for more.

2

Her orientest colours there,
    And essences most pure,
With sweetest perfumes hoarded were,
    All, as she thought, secure.

3

She seldom them unlocked, or used,
    But with the nicest care;   10
For, with one grain of them diffused,
    She could the world repair.

4

But likeness soon together drew
    What she did separate lay;
Of which one perfect beauty grew,
    And that was Celia.

5

Love wisely had of long foreseen
    That he must once grow old;
And therefore stored a magazine,
    To save him from the cold.   20

6

He kept the several cells replete
    With nitre thrice refined;
The naphtha's and the sulphur's heat,
    And all that burns the mind.

7

He fortified the double gate,
    And rarely thither came;
For, with one spark of these, he straight
    All Nature could inflame.

8

Till, by vicinity so long,
    A nearer way they sought;   30
And, grown magnetically strong,
    Into each other wrought.

9

Thus all his fuel did unite
  To make one fire high:
None ever burned so hot, so bright:
  And, Celia, that am I.

10

So we alone the happy rest,
  Whilst all the world is poor,
And have within ourselves possessed
  All Love's and Nature's store.   40

The Mower against Gardens

Luxurious man, to bring his vice in use,
  Did after him the world seduce,
And from the fields the flowers and plants allure,
  Where nature was most plain and pure.
He first enclosed within the garden's square
  A dead and standing pool of air,
And a more luscious earth for them did knead,
  Which stupefied them while it fed.
The pink grew then as double as his mind;
  The nutriment did change the kind.   10
With strange perfumes he did the roses taint,
  And flowers themselves were taught to paint.
The tulip, white, did for complexion seek,
  And learned to interline its cheek:
Its onion root they then so high did hold,
  That one was for a meadow sold.
Another world was searched, through oceans new,
  To find the *marvel of Peru*.
And yet these rarities might be allowed
  To man, that sovereign thing and proud,   20
Had he not dealt between the bark and tree,
  Forbidden mixtures there to see.
No plant now knew the stock from which it came;
  He grafts upon the wild the tame:

That the uncertain and adulterate fruit
    Might put the palate in dispute.
His green seraglio has its eunuchs too,
    Lest any tyrant him outdo.
And in the cherry he does nature vex,
    To procreate without a sex.   30
'Tis all enforced, the fountain and the grot,
    While the sweet fields do lie forgot:
Where willing nature does to all dispense
    A wild and fragrant innocence:
And fauns and fairies do the meadows till,
    More by their presence than their skill.
Their statues, polished by some ancient hand,
    May to adorn the gardens stand:
But howsoe'er the figures do excel,
    The gods themselves with us do dwell.   40

Damon the Mower

1

Hark how the Mower Damon sung,
With love of Juliana stung!
While everything did seem to paint
The scene more fit for his complaint.
Like her fair eyes the day was fair,
But scorching like his amorous care.
Sharp like his scythe his sorrow was,
And withered like his hopes the grass.

2

'Oh what unusual heats are here,
Which thus our sunburned meadows sear!   10
The grasshopper its pipe gives o'er;
And hamstringed frogs can dance no more.
But in the brook the green frog wades;
And grasshoppers seek out the shades.
Only the snake, that kept within,
Now glitters in its second skin.

3

'This heat the sun could never raise,
Nor Dog Star so inflame the days.
It from a higher beauty groweth,
Which burns the fields and mower both: 20
Which mads the dog, and makes the sun
Hotter than his own Phaeton.
Not July causeth these extremes,
But Juliana's scorching beams.

4

'Tell me where I may pass the fires
Of the hot day, or hot desires.
To what cool cave shall I descend,
Or to what gelid fountain bend?
Alas! I look for ease in vain,
When remedies themselves complain. 30
No moisture but my tears do rest,
Nor cold but in her icy breast.

5

'How long wilt thou, fair shepherdess,
Esteem me, and my presents less?
To thee the harmless snake I bring,
Disarmed of its teeth and sting;
To thee chameleons, changing hue,
And oak leaves tipped with honey dew.
Yet thou, ungrateful, hast not sought
Nor what they are, nor who them brought. 40

6

'I am the Mower Damon, known
Through all the meadows I have mown.
On me the morn her dew distills
Before her darling daffodils.
And, if at noon my toil me heat,
The sun himself licks off my sweat.
While, going home, the evening sweet
In cowslip-water bathes my feet.

7

'What, though the piping shepherd stock
The plains with an unnumbered flock,   50
This scythe of mine discovers wide
More ground than all his sheep do hide.
With this the golden fleece I shear
Of all these closes every year.
And though in wool more poor than they,
Yet am I richer far in hay.

8

'Nor am I so deformed to sight,
If in my scythe I looked right;
In which I see my picture done,
As in a crescent moon the sun.   60
The deathless fairies take me oft
To lead them in their dances soft:
And, when I tune myself to sing,
About me they contract their ring.

9

'How happy might I still have mowed,
Had not Love here his thistles sowed!
But now I all the day complain,
Joining my labour to my pain;
And with my scythe cut down the grass,
Yet still my grief is where it was: 70
But, when the iron blunter grows,
Sighing, I whet my scythe and woes.'

10

While thus he threw his elbow round,
Depopulating all the ground,
And, with his whistling scythe, does cut
Each stroke between the earth and root,
The edged steel by careless chance
Did into his own ankle glance;
And there among the grass fell down,
By his own scythe, the Mower mown.   80

11

'Alas!' said he, 'these hurts are slight
To those that die by love's despite.
With shepherd's-purse, and clown's-all-heal,
The blood I staunch, and wound I seal.
Only for him no cure is found,
Whom Juliana's eyes do wound.
'Tis death alone that this must do:
For Death thou art a Mower too.'

The Mower to the Glow-worms

1

Ye living lamps, by whose dear light
The nightingale does sit so late,
And studying all the summer night,
Her matchless songs does meditate;

2

Ye country comets, that portend
No war, nor prince's funeral,
Shining unto no higher end
Than to presage the grass's fall;

3

Ye glow-worms, whose officious flame
To wandering mowers shows the way,   10
That in the night have lost their aim,
And after foolish fires do stray;

4

Your courteous lights in vain you waste,
Since Juliana here is come,
For she my mind hath so displaced
That I shall never find my home.

The Mower's Song

1

My mind was once the true survey
Of all these meadows fresh and gay,
And in the greenness of the grass
Did see its hopes as in a glass;
When Juliana came, and she
What I do to the grass, does to my thoughts and me.

2

But these, while I with sorrow pine,
Grew more luxuriant still and fine,
That not one blade of grass you spied,
But had a flower on either side;   10
When Juliana came, and she
What I do to the grass, does to my thoughts and me.

3

Unthankful meadows, could you so
A fellowship so true forgo,
And in your gaudy May-games meet,
While I lay trodden under feet?
When Juliana came, and she
What I do to the grass, does to my thoughts and me.

4

But what you in compassion ought,
Shall now by my revenge be wrought: 20
And flowers, and grass, and I and all,
Will in one common ruin fall.
For Juliana comes, and she
What I do to the grass, does to my thoughts and me.

5

And thus, ye meadows, which have been
Companions of my thoughts more green,
Shall now the heraldry become
With which I shall adorn my tomb;
For Juliana comes, and she
What I do to the grass, does to my thoughts and me.   30

Ametas and Thestylis making Hay-ropes

1

AMETAS

Thinkst thou that this love can stand,
Whilst thou still dost say me nay?
Love unpaid does soon disband:
Love binds love as hay binds hay.

2

THESTYLIS

Thinkst thou that this rope would twine
If we both should turn one way?
Where both parties so combine,
Neither love will twist nor hay.

3

AMETAS

Thus you vain excuses find,
Which yourselves and us delay: 10
And love ties a woman's mind
Looser than with ropes of hay.

4

THESTYLIS

What you cannot constant hope
Must be taken as you may.

5

AMETAS

Then let's both lay by our rope,
And go kiss within the hay.

Music's Empire

1

First was the world as one great cymbal made,
Where jarring winds to infant Nature played.
All music was a solitary sound,
To hollow rocks and murmuring fountains bound.

2

Jubal first made the wilder notes agree;
And Jubal tuned music's jubilee:
He called the echoes from their sullen cell,
And built the organ's city where they dwell.

3

Each sought a consort in that lovely place;
And virgin trebles wed the manly base.   10
From whence the progeny of numbers new
Into harmonious colonies withdrew.

4

Some to the lute, some to the viol went,
And others chose the cornet eloquent,
These practising the wind, and those the wire,
To sing men's triumphs, or in heaven's choir.

5

Then music, the mosaic of the air,
Did of all these a solemn noise prepare:
With which she gained the empire of the ear,
Including all between the earth and sphere.   20

6

Victorious sounds! Yet here your homage do
Unto a gentler conqueror than you:
Who though he flies the music of his praise,
Would with you heaven's hallelujahs raise.

The Garden

1

How vainly men themselves amaze
To win the palm, the oak, or bays,
And their uncessant labours see
Crowned from some single herb or tree,

Whose short and narrow verged shade
Does prudently their toils upbraid,
While all flowers and all trees do close
To weave the garlands of repose.

2

Fair Quiet, have I found thee here,
And Innocence, thy sister dear!   10
Mistaken long, I sought you then
In busy companies of men.
Your sacred plants, if here below,
Only among the plants will grow.
Society is all but rude,
To this delicious solitude.

3

No white nor red was ever seen
So amorous as this lovely green.
Fond lovers, cruel as their flame,
Cut in these trees their mistress' name.   20
Little, alas, they know, or heed,
How far these beauties hers exceed!
Fair trees! wheres'e'er your barks I wound,
No name shall but your own be found.

4

When we have run our passion's heat,
Love hither makes his best retreat.
The gods, that mortal beauty chase,
Still in a tree did end their race.
Apollo hunted Daphne so,
Only that she might laurel grow.   30
And Pan did after Syrinx speed,
Not as a nymph, but for a reed.

5

What wondrous life in this I lead!
Ripe apples drop about my head;
The luscious clusters of the vine
Upon my mouth do crush their wine;

The nectarine, and curious peach,
Into my hands themselves do reach;
Stumbling on melons, as I pass,
Ensnared with flowers, I fall on grass.   40

6

Meanwhile the mind, from pleasure less,
Withdraws into its happiness:
The mind, that ocean where each kind
Does straight its own resemblance find,
Yet it creates, transcending these,
Far other worlds, and other seas,
Annihilating all that's made
To a green thought in a green shade.

7

Here at the fountain's sliding foot,
Or at some fruit-tree's mossy root,
Casting the body's vest aside,
My soul into the boughs does glide:
There like a bird it sits, and sings,
Then whets, and combs its silver wings;
And, till prepared for longer flight,
Waves in its plumes the various light.

8

Such was that happy garden-state,
While man there walked without a mate:
After a place so pure, and sweet,
What other help could yet be meet!   60
But 'twas beyond a mortal's share
To wander solitary there:
Two paradises 'twere in one
To live in paradise alone.

9

How well the skilful gardener drew
Of flowers and herbs this dial new,
Where from above the milder sun
Does through a fragrant zodiac run;

And, as it works, the industrious bee
Computes its time as well as we. 70
How could such sweet and wholesome hours
Be reckoned but with herbs and flowers!

The second Chorus from Seneca's Tragedy 'Thyestes'

Climb at court for me that will
Tottering favour's pinnacle;
All I seek is to lie still.
Settled in some secret nest,
In calm leisure let me rest,
And far off the public stage
Pass away my silent age.
Thus when without noise, unknown,
I have lived out all my span,
I shall die, without a groan, 10
An old honest country man.
Who exposed to others' eyes,
Into his own heart ne'er pries,
Death to him's a strange surprise.

An Epitaph upon Frances Jones

Enough: and leave the rest to Fame.
'Tis to commend her but to name.
Courtship, which living she declined,
When dead to offer were unkind.
Where never any could speak ill,
Who would officious praises spill?
Nor can the truest wit or friend,
Without detracting, her commend.
To say she lived a virgin chaste,
In this age loose and all unlaced; 10
Nor was, when vice is so allowed,
Of virtue or ashamed, or proud;
That her soul was on heaven so bent;

No minute but it came and went;
That ready her last debt to pay
She summed her life up every day;
Modest as morn; as midday bright;
Gentle as evening; cool as night;
'Tis true: but all so weakly said,
'Twere more significant, *she's dead.*   20

Upon the Hill and Grove at Bilbrough

TO THE LORD FAIRFAX

1

See how the arched earth does here
Rise in a perfect hemisphere!
The stiffest compass could not strike
A line more circular and like;
Nor softest pencil draw a brow
So equal as this hill does bow.
It seems as for a model laid,
And that the world by it was made.

2

Here learn, ye mountains more unjust,
Which to abrupter greatness thrust,   10
That do with your hook-shouldered height
The earth deform and heaven fright,
For whose excrescence ill-designed,
Nature must a new centre find,
Learn here those humble steps to tread,
Which to securer glory lead.

3

See what a soft access and wide
Lies open to its grassy side;
Nor with the rugged path deters
The feet of breathless travellers.   20
See then how courteous it ascends,

And all the way it rises bends;
Nor for itself the height does gain,
But only strives to raise the plain.

4

Yet thus it all the field commands,
And in unenvied greatness stands,
Discerning further than the cliff
Of heaven-daring Tenerife.
How glad the weary seamen haste
When they salute it from the mast!   30
By night the Northern Star their way
Directs, and this no less by day.

5

Upon its crest this mountain grave
A plume of aged trees does wave.
No hostile hand durst ere invade
With impious steel the sacred shade.
For something always did appear
Of the great master's terror there:
And men could hear his armour still
Rattling through all the grove and hill.   40

6

Fear of the master, and respect
Of the great nymph, did it protect,
Vera the nymph that him inspired,
To whom he often here retired,
And on these oaks engraved her name;
Such wounds alone these woods became:
But ere he well the barks could part
'Twas writ already in their heart.

7

For they ('tis credible) have sense,
As we, of love and reverence,   50
And underneath the coarser rind
The genius of the house do bind.
Hence they successes seem to know,

And in their lord's advancement grow;
But in no memory were seen,
As under this so straight and green;

8

Yet now no further strive to shoot,
Contented if they fix their root.
Nor to the wind's uncertain gust,
Their prudent heads too far entrust.   60
Only sometimes a fluttering breeze
Discourses with the breathing trees,
Which in their modest whispers name
Those acts that swelled the cheek of fame.

9

'Much other groves', say they, 'than these
And other hills him once did please.
Through groves of pikes he thundered then,
And mountains raised of dying men.
For all the civic garlands due
To him our branches are but few.   70
Nor are our trunks enow to bear
The trophies of one fertile year.'

10

'Tis true, ye trees, nor ever spoke
More certain oracles in oak.
But peace, (if you his favour prize):
That courage its own praises flies.
Therefore to your obscurer seats
From his own brightness he retreats:
Nor he the hills without the groves,
Nor height, but with retirement, loves.   80

Upon Appleton House

TO THE LORD FAIRFAX

I

Within this sober frame expect
Work of no foreign architect,
That unto caves the quarries drew,
And forests did to pastures hew,
Who of his great design in pain
Did for a model vault his brain,
Whose columns should so high be raised
To arch the brows that on them gazed.

2

Why should of all things man unruled
Such unproportioned dwellings guild?　　　　10
The beasts are by their dens expressed:
And birds contrive an equal nest;
The low-roofed tortoises do dwell
In cases fit of tortoise shell:
No creature loves an empty space;
Their bodies measure out their place.

3

But he, superfluously spread,
Demands more room alive than dead;
And in his hollow palace goes
Where winds (as he) themselves may lose;　　　20
What need of all this marble crust
T'impark the wanton mote of dust,
That thinks by breadth the world t'unite
Though the first builders failed in height?

4

But all things are composed here
Like Nature, orderly and near:
In which we the dimensions find
Of that more sober age and mind,

When larger-sized men did stoop
To enter at a narrow loop;   30
As practising, in doors so strait,
To strain themselves through heaven's gate.

5

And surely when the after age
Shall hither come in pilgrimage,
These sacred places to adore,
By Vere and Fairfax trod before,
Men will dispute how their extent
Within such dwarfish confines went:
And some will smile at this, as well
As Romulus his bee-like cell.   40

6

Humility alone designs
Those short but admirable lines,
By which, ungirt and unconstraincd,
Things greater are in less contained.
Let others vainly strive t'immure
The circle in the quadrature!
These holy mathematics can
In every figure equal man.

7

Yet thus the laden house does sweat,
And scarce endures the master great: 50
But where he comes the swelling hall
Stirs, and the square grows spherical,
More by his magnitude distressed,
Then he is by its straitness pressed:
And too officiously it slights
That in itself which him delights.

8

So honour better lowness bears,
Than that unwonted greatness wears:
Height with a certain grace does bend,
But low things clownishly ascend.   60

And yet what needs there here excuse,
Where everything does answer use?
Where neatness nothing can condemn,
Nor pride invent what to contemn?

9

A stately frontispiece of poor
Adorns without the open door:
Nor less the rooms within commends
Daily new furniture of friends.
The house was built upon the place
Only as for a mark of grace;   70
And for an inn to entertain
Its lord a while, but not remain.

10

Him Bishop's Hill or Denton may,
Or Bilbrough, better hold than they:
But Nature here hath been so free
As if she said, 'Leave this to me.'
Art would more neatly have defaced
What she had laid so sweetly waste,
In fragrant gardens, shady woods,
Deep meadows, and transparent floods.   80

11

While with slow eyes we these survey,
And on each pleasant footstep stay,
We opportunely may relate
The progress of this house's fate.
A nunnery first gave it birth
(For virgin buildings oft brought forth);
And all that neighbour-ruin shows
The quarries whence this dwelling rose.

12

Near to this gloomy cloister's gates
There dwelt the blooming virgin Thwaites,   90
Fair beyond measure, and an heir
Which might deformity make fair.

And oft she spent the summer suns
Discoursing with the subtle nuns.
Whence in these words one to her weaved,
(As 'twere by chance) thoughts long conceived.

13

'Within this holy leisure we
Live innocently, as you see.
These walls restrain the world without,
But hedge our liberty about.   100
These bars enclose that wider den
Of those wild creatures called men.
The cloister outward shuts its gates,
And, from us, locks on them the grates.

14

'Here we, in shining armour white,
Like virgin Amazons do fight.
And our chaste lamps we hourly trim,
Lest the great bridegroom find them dim.
Our orient breaths perfumed are
With incense of incessant prayer.   110
And holy-water of our tears
Most strangely our complexion clears.

15

'Not tears of grief; but such as those
With which calm pleasure overflows;
Or pity, when we look on you
That live without this happy vow.
How should we grieve that must be seen
Each one a spouse, and each a queen,
And can in heaven hence behold
Our brighter robes and crowns of gold?   120

16

'When we have prayed all our beads,
Some on the holy legend reads;
While all the rest with needles paint
The face and graces of the saint.

But what the linen can't receive
They in their lives do interweave.
This work the saints best represents;
That serves for altar's ornaments.

17

'But much it to our work would add
If here your hand, your face we had: 130
By it we would Our Lady touch;
Yet thus she you resembles much.
Some of your features, as we sewed,
Through every shrine should be bestowed.
And one in beauty we would take
Enough a thousand saints to make.

18

'And (for I dare not quench the fire
That me does for your good inspire)
'Twere sacrilege a man t'admit
To holy things, for heaven fit.   140
I see the angels in a crown
On you the lilies showering down:
And around about you glory breaks,
That something more than human speaks.

19

'All beauty, when at such a height,
Is so already consecrate.
Fairfax I know; and long ere this
Have marked the youth, and what he is.
But can he such a rival seem
For whom you heaven should disesteem?   150
Ah, no! and 'twould more honour prove
He your *devoto* were, than love.

20

'Here live beloved, and obeyed:
Each one your sister, each your maid.
And, if our rule seem strictly penned,
The rule itself to you shall bend.

Our abbess too, now far in age,
Doth your succession near presage.
How soft the yoke on us would lie
Might such fair hands as yours it tie!   160

21

'Your voice, the sweetest of the choir,
Shall draw heaven nearer, raise us higher.
And your example, if our head,
Will soon us to perfection lead.
Those virtues to us all so dear,
Will straight grow sanctity when here:
And that, once sprung, increase so fast
Till miracles it work at last.

22

'Nor is our order yet so nice,
Delight to banish as a vice.   170
Here pleasure piety doth meet;
One perfecting the other sweet.
So through the mortal fruit we boil
The sugar's uncorrupting oil:
And that which perished while we pull,
Is thus preserved clear and full.

23

'For such indeed are all our arts,
Still handling Nature's finest parts.
Flowers dress the altars; for the clothes,
The sea-born amber we compose;   180
Balms for the grieved we draw; and pastes
We mold, as baits for curious tastes.
What need is here of man? unless
These as sweet sins we should confess.

24

'Each night among us to your side
Appoint a fresh and virgin bride;
Whom if our Lord at midnight find,
Yet neither should be left behind.

Where you may lie as chaste in bed,
As pearls together billeted,   190
All night embracing arm in arm
Like crystal pure with cotton warm.

25

'But what is this to all the store
Of joys you see, and may make more!
Try but a while, if you be wise:
The trial neither costs, nor ties.'
Now, Fairfax, seek her promised faith:
Religion that dispensed hath,
Which she henceforward does begin;
The nun's smooth tongue has sucked her in.   200

26

Oft, though he knew it was in vain,
Yet would he valiantly complain.
'Is this that sanctity so great,
An art by which you finelier cheat?
Hypocrite witches, hence avaunt,
Who though in prison yet enchant!
Death only can such thieves make fast,
As rob though in the dungeon cast.

27

'Were there but, when this house was made,
One stone that a just hand had laid,   210
It must have fall'n upon her head
Who first thee from thy faith misled.
And yet, how well soever meant,
With them 'twould soon grow fraudulent;
For like themselves they alter all,
And vice infects the very wall.

28

'But sure those buildings last not long,
Founded by folly, kept by wrong.
I know what fruit their gardens yield,
When they it think by night concealed.   220

Fly from their vices. 'Tis thy state,
Not thee, that they would consecrate.
Fly from their ruin. How I fear,
Though guiltless, lest thou perish there.'

29

What should he do? He would respect
Religion, but not right neglect:
For first religion taught him right,
And dazzled not but cleared his sight.
Sometimes resolved, his sword he draws,
But reverenceth then the laws: 230
For justice still that courage led;
First from a judge, then soldier bred.

30

Small honour would be in the storm.
The court him grants the lawful form;
Which licensed either peace or force,
To hinder the unjust divorce.
Yet still the nuns his right debarred,
Standing upon their holy guard.
Ill-counselled women, do you know
Whom you resist, or what you do?   240

31

Is not this he whose offspring fierce
Shall fight through all the universe;
And with successive valour try
France, Poland, either Germany;
Till one, as long since prophesied,
His horse through conquered Britain ride?
Yet, against fate, his spouse they kept,
And the great race would intercept.

32

Some to the breach against their foes
Their wooden saints in vain oppose.   250
Another bolder stands at push
With their old holy-water brush.

While the disjointed abbess threads
The jingling chain-shot of her beads.
But their loudest cannon were their lungs;
And sharpest weapons were their tongues.

33

But waving these aside like flies,
Young Fairfax through the wall does rise.
Then th' unfrequented vault appeared,
And superstitions vainly feared.   260
The relics false were set to view;
Only the jewels there were true—
But truly bright and holy Thwaites
That weeping at the altar waits.

34

But the glad youth away her bears,
And to the nuns bequeaths her tears;
Who guiltily their prize bemoan,
Like gypsies that a child had stolen.
Thenceforth (as when the enchantment ends,
The castle vanishes or rends)   270
The wasting cloister with the rest
Was in one instant dispossessed.

35

At the demolishing, this seat
To Fairfax fell as by escheat.
And what both nuns and founders willed
'Tis likely better thus fulfilled.
For if the virgin proved not theirs,
The cloister yet remained hers.
Though many a nun there made her vow,
'Twas no religious house till now.   280

36

From that blest bed the hero came,
Whom France and Poland yet does fame:
Who, when retired here to peace,
His warlike studies could not cease;

But laid these gardens out in sport
In the just figure of a fort;
And with five bastions it did fence,
As aiming one for every sense.

37

When in the east the morning ray
Hangs out the colours of the day,   290
The bee through these known alleys hums,
Beating the *dian* with its drums.
Then flowers their drowsy eyelids raise,
Their silken ensigns each displays,
And dries its pan yet dank with dew,
And fills its flask with odours new.

38

These, as their governor goes by,
In fragrant volleys they let fly;
And to salute their governess
Again as great a charge they press: 300
None for the virgin nymph; for she
Seems with the flowers a flower to be.
And think so still! though not compare
With breath so sweet, or cheek so fair.

39

Well shot, ye firemen! Oh how sweet,
And round your equal fires do meet,
Whose shrill report no ear can tell,
But echoes to the eye and smell.
See how the flowers, as at parade,
Under their colours stand displayed: 310
Each regiment in order grows,
That of the tulip, pink, and rose.

40

But when the vigilant patrol
Of stars walks round about the Pole,
Their leaves, that to the stalks are curled,
Seem to their staves the ensigns furled.

Then in some flower's beloved hut
Each bee as sentinel is shut,
And sleeps so too: but, if once stirred,
She runs you through, or asks the word. 320

41

Oh thou, that dear and happy isle
The garden of the world ere while,
Thou paradise of four seas,
Which heaven planted us to please,
But, to exclude the world, did guard
With watery if not flaming sword;
What luckless apple did we taste,
To make us mortal, and thee waste?

42

Unhappy! shall we never more
That sweet militia restore, 330
When gardens only had their towers,
And all the garrisons were flowers,
When roses only arms might bear,
And men did rosy garlands wear?
Tulips, in several colours barred,
Were then the Switzers of our Guard.

43

The gardener had the soldier's place,
And his more gentle forts did trace.
The nursery of all things green
Was then the only magazine. 340
The winter quarters were the stoves,
Where he the tender plants removes.
But war all this doth overgrow;
We ordnance plant and powder sow.

44

And yet their walks one on the sod
Who, had it pleased him and God,
Might once have made our gardens spring
Fresh as his own and flourishing.

But he preferred to the Cinque Ports
These five imaginary forts,   350
And, in those half-dry trenches, spanned
Power which the ocean might command.

45

For he did, with his utmost skill,
Ambition weed, but conscience till—
Conscience, that heaven-nursed plant,
Which most our earthy gardens want.
A prickling leaf it bears, and such
As that which shrinks at every touch;
But flowers eternal, and divine,
That in the crowns of saints do shine.   360

46

The sight does from these bastions ply,
The invisible artillery;
And at proud Cawood Castle seems
To point the battery of its beams.
As if it quarrelled in the seat
The ambition of its prelate great.
But o'er the meads below it plays,
Or innocently seems to gaze.

47

And now to the abyss I pass
Of that unfathomable grass,   370
Where men like grasshoppers appear,
But grasshoppers are giants there:
They, in their squeaking laugh, contemn
Us as we walk more low than them:
And, from the precipices tall
Of the green spires, to us do call.

48

To see men through this meadow dive,
We wonder how they rise alive,
As, under water, none does know
Whether he fall through it or go.   380

But, as the mariners that sound,
And show upon their lead the ground,
They bring up flowers so to be seen,
And prove they've at the bottom been.

49

No scene that turns with engines strange
Does oftener than these meadows change.
For when the sun the grass hath vexed,
The tawny mowers enter next;
Who seem like Israelites to be,
Walking on foot through a green sea.   390
To them the grassy deeps divide,
And crowd a lane to either side.

50

With whistling scythe, and elbow strong,
These massacre the grass along:
While one, unknowing, carves the rail,
Whose yet unfeathered quills her fail.
The edge all bloody from its breast
He draws, and does his stroke detest,
Fearing the flesh untimely mowed
To him a fate as black forebode.   400

51

But bloody Thestylis, that waits
To bring the mowing camp their cates,
Greedy as kites, has trussed it up,
And forthwith means on it to sup:
When on another quick she lights,
And cries, 'He called us Israelites;
But now, to make his saying true,
Rails rain for quails, for manna, dew.'

52

Unhappy birds! what does it boot
To build below the grass's root;
When lowness is unsafe as height,   410
And chance o'ertakes, what 'scapeth spite?

And now your orphan parents' call
Sounds your untimely funeral.
Death-trumpets creak in such a note,
And 'tis the sourdine in their throat.

53

Or sooner hatch or higher build:
The mower now commands the field,
In whose new traverse seemeth wrought
A camp of battle newly fought: 420
Where, as the meads with hay, the plain
Lies quilted o'er with bodies slain:
The women that with forks it fling,
Do represent the pillaging.

54

And now the careless victors play,
Dancing the triumphs of the hay;
Where every mower's wholesome heat
Smells like an Alexander's sweat.
Their females fragrant as the mead
Which they in fairy circles tread: 430
When at their dance's end they kiss,
Their new-made hay not sweeter is.

55

When after this 'tis piled in cocks,
Like a calm sea it shows the rocks,
We wondering in the river near
How boats among them safely steer.
Or, like the desert Memphis sand,
Short pyramids of hay do stand.
And such the Roman camps do rise
In hills for soldiers' obsequies.   440

56

This scene again withdrawing brings
A new and empty face of things,
A levelled space, as smooth and plain
As cloths for Lely stretched to stain.

The world when first created sure
Was such a table rase and pure.
Or rather such is the *toril*
Ere the bulls enter at Madril.

57

For to this naked equal flat,
Which Levellers take pattern at,   450
The villagers in common chase
Their cattle, which it closer rase;
And what below the scythe increased
Is pinched yet nearer by the beast.
Such, in the painted world, appeared
Davenant with the universal herd.

58

They seem within the polished grass
A landskip drawn in looking-glass,
And shrunk in the huge pasture show
As spots, so shaped, on faces do—   460
Such fleas, ere they approach the eye,
In multiplying glasses lie.
They feed so wide, so slowly move,
As constellations do above.

59

Then, to conclude these pleasant acts,
Denton sets ope its cataracts,
And makes the meadow truly be
(What it but seemed before) a sea.
For, jealous of its lord's long stay,
It tries t'invite him thus away.   470
The river in itself is drowned,
And isles the astonished cattle round.

60

Let others tell the paradox,
How eels now bellow in the ox;
How horses at their tails do kick,
Turned as they hang to leeches quick;

How boats can over bridges sail;
And fishes do the stables scale.
How salmons trespassing are found;
And pikes are taken in the pound.   480

61

But I, retiring from the flood,
Take sanctuary in the wood,
And, while it lasts, myself embark
In this yet green, yet growing ark,
Where the first carpenter might best
Fit timber for his keel have pressed.
And where all creatures might have shares,
Although in armies, not in pairs.

62

The double wood of ancient stocks,
Linked in so thick, a union locks,   490
It like two pedigrees appears,
On th'one hand Fairfax, th' other Vere's:
Of whom though many fell in war,
Yet more to heaven shooting are:
And, as they Nature's cradle decked,
Will in green age her hearse expect.

63

When first the eye this forest sees
It seems indeed as wood not trees:
As if their neighbourhood so old
To one great trunk them all did mould.   500
There the huge bulk takes place, as meant
To thrust up a fifth element,
And stretches still so closely wedged
As if the night within were hedged.

64

Dark all without its knits; within
It opens passable and thin;
And in as loose an order grows,
As the Corinthian porticoes.

The arching boughs unite between
The columns of the temple green; 510
And underneath the winged choirs
Echo about their tuned fires.

65

The nightingale does here make choice
To sing the trials of her voice.
Low shrubs she sits in, and adorns
With music high the squatted thorns.
But highest oaks stoop down to hear,
And listening elders prick the ear.
The thorn, lest it should hurt her, draws
Within the skin its shrunken claws. 520

66

But I have for my music found
A sadder, yet more pleasing sound:
The stockdoves, whose fair necks are graced
With nuptial rings, their ensigns chaste;
Yet always, for some cause unknown,
Sad pair unto the elms they moan.
O why should such a couple mourn,
That in so equal flames do burn!

67

Then as I careless on the bed
Of gelid strawberries do tread, 530
And through the hazels thick espy
The hatching throstle's shining eye,
The heron from the ash's top,
The eldest of its young lets drop,
As if it stork-like did pretend
That tribute to its lord to send.

68

But most the hewel's wonders are,
Who here has the holt-felster's care.
He walks still upright from the root,
Measuring the timber with his foot, 540

And all the way, to keep it clean,
Doth from the bark the woodmoths glean.
He, with his beak, examines well
Which fit to stand and which to fell.

69

The good he numbers up, and hacks,
As if he marked them with the axe,
But where he, tinkling with his beak,
Does find the hollow oak to speak,
That for his building he designs,
And through the tainted side he mines.   550
Who could have thought the tallest oak
Should fall by such a feeble stroke!

70

Nor would it, had the tree not fed
A traitor-worm, within it bred,
(As first our flesh corrupt within
Tempts impotent and bashful sin).
And yet that worm triumphs not long,
But serves to feed the hewel's young,
While the oak seems to fall content,
Viewing the treason's punishment.   560

71

Thus I, easy philosopher,
Among the birds and trees confer.
And little now to make me wants
Or of the fowls, or of the plants:
Give me but wings as they, and I
Straight floating on the air shall fly:
Or turn me but, and you shall see
I was but an inverted tree.

72

Already I begin to call
In their most learned original: 570
And where I language want, my signs
The bird upon the bough divines;

And more attentive there doth sit
Than if she were with lime-twigs knit.
No leaf does tremble in the wind
Which I, returning, cannot find.

73

Out of these scattered Sibyl's leaves
Strange prophecies my fancy weaves:
And in one history consumes,
Like Mexique paintings, all the plumes.   580
What Rome, Greece, Palestine, ere said
I in this light mosaic read.
Thrice happy he who, not mistook,
Hath read in Nature's mystic book.

74

And see how chance's better wit
Could with a mask my studies hit!
The oak leaves me embroider all,
Between which caterpillars crawl:
And ivy, with familiar trails,
Me licks, and clasps, and curls, and hales.   590
Under this antic cope I move
Like some great prelate of the grove.

75

Then, languishing with ease, I toss
On pallets swoll'n of velvet moss,
While the wind, cooling through the boughs,
Flatters with air my panting brows.
Thanks for my rest, ye mossy banks;
And unto you, cool zephyrs, thanks,
Who, as my hair, my thoughts too shed,
And winnow from the chaff my head.   600

76

How safe, methinks, and strong, behind
These trees have I encamped my mind:
Where beauty, aiming at the heart,
Bends in some tree its useless dart;

And where the world no certain shot
Can make, or me it toucheth not.
But I on it securely play,
And gall its horsemen all the day.

77

Bind me, ye woodbines, in your twines,
Curl me about, ye gadding vines,   610
And, oh, so close your circles lace,
That I may never leave this place:
But lest your fetters prove too weak,
Ere I your silken bondage break,
Do you, O brambles, chain me too,
And, courteous briars, nail me through.

78

Here in the morning tie my chain,
Where the two woods have made a lane,
While, like a guard on either side,
The trees before their lord divide;   620
This, like a long and equal thread,
Betwixt two labyrinths does lead.
But where the floods did lately drown,
There at the evening stake me down.

79

For now the waves are fall'n and dried,
And now the meadows fresher dyed,
Whose grass, with moister colour dashed,
Seems as green silks but newly washed.
No serpent new nor crocodile
Remains behind our little Nile,   630
Unless itself you will mistake,
Among these meads the only snake.

80

See in what wanton harmless folds
It everywhere the meadow holds;
And its yet muddy back doth lick,
Till as a crystal mirror slick,

Where all things gaze themselves, and doubt
If they be in it or without.
And for his shade which therein shines,
Narcissus-like, the sun too pines.   640

81

Oh what a pleasure 'tis to hedge
My temples here with heavy sedge,
Abandoning my lazy side,
Stretched as a bank unto the tide,
Or to suspend my sliding foot
On th'osier's undermined root,
And in its branches tough to hang,
While at my lines the fishes twang!

82

But now away my hooks, my quills,
And angles—idle utensils.   650
The young Maria walks tonight:
Hide, trifling youth, thy pleasures slight.
'Twere shame that such judicious eyes
Should with such toys a man surprise;
She, that already is the law
Of all her sex, her age's awe.

83

See how loose Nature, in respect
To her, itself doth recollect;
And everything so whisht and fine,
Starts forthwith to its *bonne mine*.   660
The sun himself, or her aware,
Seems to descend with greater care;
And lest she see him go to bed,
In blushing clouds conceals his head.

84

So when the shadows laid asleep
From underneath these banks do creep,
And on the river as it flows
With eben shuts begin to close;

The modest halcyon comes in sight,
Flying betwixt the day and night;   670
And such a horror calm and dumb,
Admiring Nature does benumb.

85

The viscous air, wheres'e'er she fly,
Follows and sucks her azure dye;
The jellying stream compacts below,
If it might fix her shadow so;
The stupid fishes hang, as plain
As flies in crystal overta'en;
And men the silent scene assist,
Charmed with the sapphire-winged mist.   680

86

Maria such, and so doth hush
The world, and through the evening rush.
No new-born comet such a train
Draws through the sky, nor star new-slain.
For straight those giddy rockets fail,
Which from the putrid earth exhale,
But by her flames, in heaven tried,
Nature is wholly vitrified.

87

'Tis she that to these gardens gave
That wondrous beauty which they have;   690
She straightness on the woods bestows;
To her the meadow sweetness owes;
Nothing could make the river be
So crystal pure but only she;
She yet more pure, sweet, straight, and fair,
Than gardens, woods, meads, rivers are.

88

Therefore what first she on them spent,
They gratefully again present:
The meadow, carpets where to tread;
The garden, flow'rs to crown her head;   700

And for a glass, the limpid brook,
Where she may all her beauties look;
But, since she would not have them seen,
The wood about her draws a screen.

89

For she, to higher beauties raised,
Disdains to be for lesser praised.
She counts her beauty to converse
In all the languages as hers;
Nor yet in those herself employs
But for the wisdom, not the noise;   710
Nor yet that wisdom would affect,
But as 'tis heaven's dialect.

90

Blest nymph! that couldst so soon prevent
Those trains by youth against thee meant:
Tears (watery shot that pierce the mind);
And signs (love's cannon charged with wind);
True praise (that breaks through all defence);
And feigned complying innocence;
But knowing where this ambush lay,
She 'scaped the safe, but roughest way.   720

91

This 'tis to have been from the first
In a domestic heaven nursed,
Under the discipline severe
Of Fairfax, and the starry Vere;
Where not one object can come nigh
But pure, and spotless as the eye;
And goodness doth itself entail
On females, if there want a male.

92

Go now, fond sex, that on your face
Do all your useless study place,   730
Nor once at vice your brows dare knit
Lest the smooth forehead wrinkled sit:

Yet your own face shall at you grin,
Thorough the black-bag of your skin,
When knowledge only could have filled
And virtue all those furrows tilled.

93

Hence she with graces more divine
Supplies beyond her sex the line;
And like a sprig of mistletoe
On the Fairfacian oak does grow;   740
Whence, for some universal good,
The priest shall cut the sacred bud,
While her glad parents most rejoice,
And make their destiny their choice.

94

Meantime, ye fields, springs, bushes, flowers,
Where yet she leads her studious hours,
(Till fate her worthily translates,
And find a Fairfax for our Thwaites),
Employ the means you have by her,
And in your kind yourselves prefer;   750
That, as all virgins she precedes,
So you all woods, streams, gardens, meads.

95

For you, Thessalian Tempe's seat
Shall now be scorned as obsolete;
Aranjuez, as less, disdained;
The Bel-Retiro as constrained;
But name not the Idalian grove—
For 'twas the seat of wanton love—
Much less the dead's Elysian Fields,
Yet nor to them your beauty yields.   760

96

'Tis not, what once it was, the world,
But a rude heap together hurled,
All negligently overthrown,
Gulfs, deserts, precipices, stone.

Your lesser world contains the same,
But in more decent order tame;
You, heaven's centre, Nature's lap,
And paradise's only map.

                    97

But now the salmon-fishers moist
Their leathern boats begin to hoist,   770
And like Antipodes in shoes,
Have shod their heads in their canoes.
How tortoise-like, but not so slow,
These rational amphibii go!
Let's in: for the dark hemisphere
Does now like one of them appear.

Flecknoe, an English Priest at Rome

Obliged by frequent visits of this man,
Whom as priest, poet, and musician,
I for some branch of Melchizedek took
(Though he derives himself from 'my Lord Brooke');
I sought his lodging, which is at the sign
Of The Sad Pelican—subject divine
For poetry. There, three staircases high—
Which signifies his triple property—
I found at last a chamber, as 'twas said,
But seemed a coffin set on the stairs' head   10
Not higher than seven, nor larger than three feet;
Only there was nor ceiling, nor a sheet,
Save that the ingenious door did, as you come,
Turn in, and show to wainscot half the room.
Yet of his state no man could have complained,
There being no bed where he entertained:
And though within one cell so narrow pent,
He'd stanzas for a whole *appartement*.
  Straight without further information,
In hideous verse, he, and a dismal tone,   20
Begins to exorcise, as if I were
Possessed; and sure the Devil brought me there.

But I, who now imagined myself brought
To my last trial, in a serious thought
Calmed the disorders of my youthful breast,
And to my martyrdom prepared rest.
Only this frail ambition did remain,
The last distemper of the sober brain,
That there had been some present to assure
The future ages how I did endure: 30
And how I, silent, turned my burning ear
Towards the verse; and when that could not hear,
Held him the other; and unchanged yet,
Asked still for more, and prayed him to repeat:
Till the tyrant, weary to persecute,
Left off, and tried to allure me with his lute.

Now as two instruments, to the same key
Being tuned by art, if the one touched be
The other opposite as soon replies,
Moved by the air and hidden sympathies;   40
So while he with his gouty fingers crawls
Over the lute, his murmuring belly calls,
Whose hungry guts to the same straitness twined
In echo to the trembling strings repined.

I, that perceived now what his music meant,
Asked civilly if he had eat this Lent.
He answered yes, with such and such an one.
For he has this of generous, that alone
He never feeds, save only when he tries
With gristly tongue to dart the passing flies.   50
I asked if he eat flesh. And he, that was
So hungry that, though ready to say mass,
Would break his fast before, said he was sick,
And the ordinance was only politic.
Nor was I longer to invite him scant,
Happy at once to make him Protestant,
And silent. Nothing now our dinner stayed
But till he had himself a body made—
I mean till he were dressed: for else so thin
He stands, as if he only fed had been   60
With consecrated wafers: and the host
Hath sure more flesh and blood than he can boast.
This *basso relievo* of a man,

Who as a camel tall, yet easily can
The needle's eye thread without any stitch,
(His only impossible is to be rich),
Lest his too subtle body, growing rare,
Should leave his soul to wander in the air,
He therefore circumscribes himself in rhymes;
And swaddled in's own papers seven times,   70
Wears a close jacket of poetic buff,
With which he doth his third dimension stuff.
Thus armed underneath, he over all
Does make a primitive *sottana* fall;
And above that yet casts an antic cloak,
Worn at the first Council of Antioch,
Which by the Jews long hid, and disesteemed,
He heard of by tradition, and redeemed.
But were he not in this black habit decked,
This half-transparent man would soon reflect   80
Each colour that he passed by, and be seen,
As the chameleon, yellow, blue, or green.
   He dressed, and ready to disfurnish now
His chamber, whose compactness did allow
No empty place for complimenting doubt,
But who came last is forced first to go out;
I meet one on the stairs who made me stand,
Stopping the passage, and did him demand.
I answered, 'He is here, Sir; but you see
You cannot pass to him but thorough me.'   90
He thought himself affronted, and replied,
'I whom the palace never has denied
Will make the way here;' I said, 'Sir, you'll do
Me a great favour, for I seek to go.'
He gathering fury still made sign to draw;
But himself there closed in a scabbard saw
As narrow as his sword's; and I, that was
Delightful, said, 'There can no body pass
Except by penetration hither, where
Two make a crowd; nor can three persons here   100
Consist but in one substance.' Then, to fit
Our peace, the priest said I too had some wit.
To prov't, I said, 'The place doth us invite
By its own narrowness, Sir, to unite.'

He asked me pardon; and to make me way
Went down, as I him followed to obey.
But the propitiatory priest had straight
Obliged us, when below, to celebrate
Together our atonement: so increased
Betwixt us two the dinner to a feast.   110
   Let it suffice that we could eat in peace;
And that both poems did and quarrels cease
During the table; though my new-made friend
Did, as he threatened, ere 'twere long intend
To be both witty and valiant: I, loath,
Said 'twas too late, he was already both.
   But now, alas, my first tormentor came,
Who satisfied with eating, but not tame,
Turns to recite; though judges most severe
After the assize's dinner mild appear,   120
And on full stomach do condemn but few,
Yet he more strict my sentence doth renew,
And draws out of the black box of his breast
Ten quire of paper in which he was dressed.
Yet that which was a greater cruelty
Than Nero's poem, he calls charity:
And so the pelican at his door hung
Picks out the tender bosom to its young.
   Of all his poems there he stands ungirt
Save only two foul copies for his shirt: 130
Yet these he promises as soon as clean.
But how I loathed to see my neighbour glean
Those papers which he peeled from within
Like white flakes rising from a leper's skin!
More odious than those rags which the French youth
At ordinaries after dinner show'th
When they compare their chancres and poulains.
Yet he first kissed them, and after takes pains
To read; and then, because he understood
Not one word, thought and swore that they were good.   140
But all his praises could not now appease
The provoked author, whom it did displease
To hear his verses, by so just a curse,
That were ill made, condemned to be read worse;
And how (impossible) he made yet more

Absurdities in them than were before.
For he his untuned voice did fall or raise
As a deaf man upon a viol plays,
Making the half points and the periods run
Confuseder than the atoms in the sun.   150
Thereat the poet swelled, with anger full,
And roared out, like Perillus in's own bull:
'Sir, you read false.' 'That, any one but you,
Should know the contrary.' Whereat, I, now
Made mediator, in my room, said, 'Why,
To say that you read false, Sir, is no lie.'
Thereat the waxen youth relented straight;
But saw with sad despair that 'twas too late.
For the disdainful poet was retired
Home, his most furious satire to have fired   160
Against the rebel, who, at this struck dead,
Wept bitterly as disinherited.
Who should commend his mistress now? Or who
Praise him? Both difficult indeed to do
With truth. I counselled him to go in time,
Ere the fierce poet's anger turned to rhyme.
   He hasted; and I, finding myself free,
As one scaped strangely from captivity,
Have made the chance be painted; and go now
To hang it in Saint Peter's for a vow.   170

An Horatian Ode upon Cromwell's Return
from Ireland

The forward youth that would appear
Must now forsake his muses dear,
   Nor in the shadows sing
   His numbers languishing.
'Tis time to leave the books in dust,
And oil the unused armour's rust:
   Removing from the wall
   The corslet of the hall.
So restless Cromwell could not cease
In the inglorious arts of peace,   10

But through adventurous war
Urged his active star.
And, like the three-forked lightning, first
Breaking the clouds where it was nursed,
    Did thorough his own side
    His fiery way divide.
(For 'tis all one to courage high
The emulous or enemy:
    And with such to enclose
    Is more than to oppose.)   20
Then burning through the air he went,
And palaces and temples rent:
    And Caesar's head at last
    Did through his laurels blast.
'Tis madness to resist or blame
The force of angry heaven's flame:
    And, if we would speak true,
    Much to the man is due,
Who, from his private gardens, where
He lived reserved and austere,   30
    As if his highest plot
    To plant the bergamot,
Could by industrious valour climb
To ruin the great work of time,
    And cast the kingdom old
    Into another mould.
Though justice against fate complain,
And plead the ancient rights in vain:
    But those do hold or break
    As men are strong or weak.   40
Nature, that hateth emptiness,
Allows of penetration less:
    And therefore must make room
    Where greater spirits come.
What field of all the Civil Wars,
Where his were not the deepest scars?
    And Hampton shows what part
    He had of wiser art,
Where, twining subtile fears with hope,
He wove a net of such a scope,   50
    That Charles himself might chase

To Carisbrooke's narrow case:
That thence the royal actor borne
The tragic scaffold might adorn:
   While round the armed bands
   Did clap their bloody hands.
He nothing common did or mean
Upon that memorable scene:
   But with his keener eye
   The axe's edge did try: 60
Nor called the gods with vulgar spite
To vindicate his helpless right,
   But bowed his comely head
   Down as upon a bed.
This was that memorable hour
Which first assured the forced power.
   So when they did design
   The Capitol's first line,
A bleeding head where they begun,
Did fright the architects to run;   70
   And yet in that the State
   Foresaw its happy fate.
And now the Irish are ashamed
To see themselves in one year tamed:
   So much one man can do,
   That does both act and know.
They can affirm his praises best,
And have, though overcome, confessed
   How good he is, how just,
   And fit for highest trust: 80
Nor yet grown stiffer with command,
But still in the Republic's hand:
   How fit he is to sway
   That can so well obey.
He to the Commons' feet presents
A kingdom, for his first year's rents:
   And, what he may, forbears
   His fame, to make it theirs:
And has his sword and spoils ungirt,
To lay them at the public's skirt.   90
   So when the falcon high
   Falls heavy from the sky,

She, having killed, no more does search
But on the next green bough to perch,
   Where, when he first does lure,
   The falconer has her sure.
What may not then our isle presume
While Victory his crest does plume?
   What may not others fear
   If thus he crown each year?   100
A Caesar, he, ere long to Gaul,
To Italy a Hannibal,
   And to all states not free
   Shall climacteric be.
The Pict no shelter now shall find
Within his parti-coloured mind,
   But from this valour sad
   Shrink underneath the plaid:
Happy, if in the tufted brake
The English hunter him mistake,   110
   Nor lay his hounds in near
   The Caledonian deer.
But thou, the Wars' and Fortune's son,
March indefatigably on,
   And for the last effect
   Still keep thy sword erect:
Besides the force it has to fright
The spirits of the shady night,
   The same arts that did gain
   A power, must it maintain.   120

Tom May's Death

As one put drunk into the packet-boat,
Tom May was hurried hence and did not know't.
But was amazed on the Elysian side,
And with an eye uncertain, gazing wide,
Could not determine in what place he was,
(For whence, in Stephen's Alley, trees or grass?)
Nor where The Pope's Head, nor The Mitre lay,
Signs by which still he found and lost his way.

At last while doubtfully he all compares,
He saw near hand, as he imagined, Ares.   10
Such did he seem for corpulence and port,
But 'twas a man much of another sort;
'Twas Ben that in the dusky laurel shade
Amongst the chorus of old poets layed,
Sounding of ancient heroes, such as were
The subjects' safety, and the rebels' fear,
But how a double-headed vulture eats
Brutus and Cassius, the people's cheats.
But seeing May, he varied straight his song,
Gently to signify that he was wrong.   20
'Cups more than civil of Emathian wine,
I sing' (said he) 'and the Pharsalian Sign,
Where the historian of the commonwealth
In his own bowels sheathed the conquering health.'
By this, May to himself and them was come,
He found he was translated, and by whom,
Yet then with foot as stumbling as his tongue
Pressed for his place among the learned throng.
But Ben, who knew not neither foe nor friend,
Sworn enemy to all that do pretend,   30
Rose; more than ever he was seen severe,
Shook his gray locks, and his own bays did tear
At this intrusion. Then with laurel wand—
The awful sign of his supreme command,
At whose dread whisk Virgil himself does quake,
And Horace patiently its stroke does take—
As he crowds in, he whipped him o'er the pate
Like Pembroke at the masque, and then did rate:
  'Far from these blessed shades tread back again
Most servile wit, and mercenary pen,   40
Polydore, Lucan, Alan, Vandal, Goth,
Malignant poet and historian both,
Go seek the novice statesmen, and obtrude
On them some Roman-cast similitude,
Tell them of liberty, the stories fine,
Until you all grow consuls in your wine;
Or thou, Dictator of the glass, bestow
On him the Cato, this the Cicero,
Transferring old Rome hither in your talk,

As Bethlem's House did to Loreto walk.   50
Foul architect, that hadst not eye to see
How ill the measures of these states agree,
And who by Rome's example England lay,
Those but to Lucan do continue May.
But thee nor ignorance nor seeming good
Misled, but malice fixed and understood.
Because some one than thee more worthy wears
The sacred laurel, hence are all these tears?
Must therefore all the world be set on flame,
Because a gazette-writer missed his aim?   60
And for a tankard-bearing muse must we
As for the basket, Guelphs and Ghibellines be?
When the sword glitters o'er the judge's head,
And fear has coward churchmen silenced,
Then is the poet's time, 'tis then he draws,
And single fights forsaken virtue's cause.
He, when the wheel of empire whirleth back,
And though the world's disjointed axle crack,
Sings still of ancient rights and better times,
Seeks wretched good, arraigns successful crimes.   70
But thou, base man, first prostituted hast
Our spotless knowledge and the studies chaste,
Apostatizing from our arts and us,
To turn the chronicler to Spartacus.
Yet wast thou taken hence with equal fate,
Before thou couldst great Charles's death relate.
But what will deeper wound thy little mind,
Hast left surviving Davenant still behind,
Who laughs to see in this thy death renewed,
Right Roman poverty and gratitude.   80
Poor poet thou, and grateful senate they,
Who thy last reckoning did so largely pay,
And with the public gravity would come,
When thou hadst drunk thy last to lead thee home,
If that can be thy home where Spenser lies,
And reverend Chaucer, but their dust does rise
Against thee, and expels thee from their side,
As the eagle's plumes from other birds divide.
Nor here thy shade must dwell. Return, return,
Where sulphury Phlegethon does ever burn.   90

Thee Cerberus with all his jaws shall gnash,
Megaera thee with all her serpents lash.
Thou riveted unto Ixion's wheel
Shalt break, and the perpetual vulture feel.
'Tis just, what torments poets e'er did feign,
Thou first historically shouldst sustain.'
    Thus, by irrevocable sentence cast,
May, only Master of these Revels, passed.
And straight he vanished in a cloud of pitch,
Such as unto the Sabbath bears the witch.   100

To his worthy Friend Doctor Witty upon his Translation of the 'Popular Errors'

Sit further, and make room for thine own fame,
Where just desert enrolls thy honoured name—
The good interpreter. Some in this task
Take off the cypress veil, but leave a mask,
Changing the Latin, but do more obscure
That sense in English which was bright and pure.
So of translators they are authors grown,
For ill translators make the book their own.
Others do strive with words and forced phrase
To add such lustre, and so many rays,   10
That but to make the vessel shining, they
Much of the precious metal rub away.
He is translation's thief that addeth more,
As much as he that taketh from the store
Of the first author. Here he maketh blots
That mends; and added beauties are but spots.
    Celia whose English doth more richly flow
Than Tagus, purer than dissolved snow,
And sweet as are her lips that speak it, she
Now learns the tongues of France and Italy;   20
But she is Celia still: no other grace
But her own smiles commend that lovely face;
Her native beauty's not Italianated,
Nor her chaste mind into the French translated:
Her thoughts are English, though her sparkling wit

With other language doth them fitly fit.
    Translators learn of her: but stay, I slide
Down into error with the vulgar tide;
Women must not teach here: the Doctor doth
Stint them to caudles, almond-milk, and broth.   30
Now I reform, and surely so will all
Whose happy eyes on thy translation fall.
I see the people hastening to thy book,
Liking themselves the worse the more they look,
And so disliking, that they nothing see
Now worth the liking, but thy book and thee.
And (if I judgement have) I censure right;
For something guides my hand that I must write.
You have translation's statutes best fulfilled,
That handling neither sully nor would gild.   40

The Character of Holland

Holland, that scarce deserves the name of land,
As but the off-scouring of the British sand;
And so much earth as was contributed
By English pilots when they heaved the lead;
Or what by th' ocean's slow alluvion fell
Of shipwrecked cockle and the mussel shell;
This indigested vomit of the sea
Fell to the Dutch by just propriety.
    Glad then, as miners that have found the ore,
They with mad labour fished the land to shore,   10
And dived as desperately for each piece
Of earth, as if't had been of ambergris,
Collecting anxiously small loads of clay,
Less than what building swallows bear away,
Or than those pills which sordid beetles roll,
Transfusing into them their dunghill soul.
    How did they rivet, with gigantic piles,
Thorough the centre their new-catched miles,
And to the stake a struggling country bound,
Where barking waves still bait the forced ground,   20
Building their watery Babel far more high

To reach the sea, than those to scale the sky.
　　Yet still his claim the injured ocean laid,
And oft at leap-frog o'er their steeples played:
As if on purpose it on land had come
To show them what's their *Mare Liberum*.
A daily deluge over them does boil;
The earth and water play at level-coil;
The fish oftimes the burger dispossessed,
And sat not as a meat but as a guest.　　　　　　30
And oft the tritons and the sea nymphs saw
Whole shoals of Dutch served up for cabillau;
Or as they over the new level ranged
For pickled herring, pickled *Heeren* changed.
Nature, it seemed, ashamed of her mistake,
Would throw their land away at duck and drake.
　　Therefore necessity, that first made kings,
Something like government among them brings.
For as with pygmies; who best kills the crane,
Among the hungry, he that treasures grain,　　　　40
Among the blind, the one-eyed blinkard reigns,
So rules among the drowned, he that drains.
Not who first see the rising sun commands,
But who could first discern the rising lands.
Who best could know to pump an earth so leak
Him they their Lord and country's Father speak.
To make a bank was a great plot of state;
Invent a shovel and be a magistrate.
Hence some small dyke-grave unperceived invades
The power, and grows, as 'twere, a King of Spades.　50
But for less envy some joint states endures,
Who look like a Commission of the Sewers.
For these Half-anders, half wet, and half dry,
Nor bear strict service, nor pure liberty.
　　'Tis probable religion after this
Came next in order, which they could not miss.
How could the Dutch but be converted, when
The Apostles were so many fishermen?
Besides, the waters of themselves did rise,
And, as their land, so them did re-baptize,　　　　60
Though herring for their god few voices missed,
And Poor-John to have been the Evangelist.

Faith, that could never twins conceive before,
Never so fertile, spawned upon this shore,
More pregnant than their Margaret, that laid down
For *Hans-in-Kelder* of a whole Hans-town.
  Sure when religion did itself embark,
And from the East would Westward steer its ark,
It struck, and splitting on this unknown ground,
Each one thence pillaged the first piece he found: 70
Hence Amsterdam, Turk–Christian–Pagan–Jew,
Staple of sects and mint of schism grew,
That bank of conscience, where not one so strange
Opinion but finds credit, and exchange.
In vain for catholics ourselves we bear;
The Universal Church is only there.
Nor can civility there want for tillage,
Where wisely for their court they chose a village.
How fit a title clothes their governors,
Themselves the *Hogs*, as all their subjects *Bores*!   80
  Let it suffice to give their country fame
That it had one Civilis called by name,
Some fifteen hundred and more years ago;
But surely never any that was so.
  See but their mermaids with their tails of fish,
Reeking at church over the chafing dish:
A vestal turf enshrined in earthen ware
Fumes through the loopholes of a wooden square.
Each to the temple with these altars tend
But still does place it at her western end,   90
While the fat steam of female sacrifice
Fills the priest's nostrils and puts out his eyes.
  Or what a spectacle the skipper gross,
A water-Hercules butter-coloss,
Tunned up with all their several towns of *Beer*,
When staggering upon some land, snick and sneer,
They try, like statuaries, if they can
Cut out each other's Athos to a man:
And carve in their large bodies, where they please,
The arms of the United Provinces.   100
  But when such amity at home is showed,
What then are their confederacies abroad?
Let this one court'sy witness all the rest:

When their whole navy they together pressed—
Not Christian captives to redeem from bands,
Or intercept the western golden sands—
No, but all ancient rights and leagues must vail,
Rather than to the English strike their sail;
To whom their weather-beaten province owes
Itself—when as some greater vessel tows   110
A cockboat tossed with the same wind and fate—
We buoyed so often up their sinking state.
   Was this *Jus Belli et Pacis?* Could this be
Cause why their burgomaster of the sea
Rammed with gun powder, flaming with brand wine,
Should raging hold his linstock to the mine,
While, with feigned treaties, they invade by stealth
Our sore new circumcised Commonwealth?
   Yet of his vain attempt no more he sees
Than of case-butter shot and bullet-cheese.   120
And the torn navy staggered with him home,
While the sea laughed itself into a foam.
'Tis true since that (as fortune kindly sports),
A wholesome danger drove us to our ports,
While half their banished keels the tempest tossed,
Half bound at home in prison to the frost:
That ours meantime at leisure might careen,
In a calm winter, under skies serene,
As the obsequious air and waters rest,
Till the dear halcyon hatch out all its nest.   130
The Commonwealth doth by its losses grow;
And, like its own seas, only ebbs to flow.
Besides, that very agitation laves,
And purges out the corruptible waves.
   And now again our armed *Bucentore*
Doth yearly their sea nuptials restore.
And now the hydra of seven provinces
Is strangled by our infant Hercules.
Their tortoise wants its vainly stretched neck;
Their navy all our conquest or our wreck;   140
Or, what is left, their Carthage overcome
Would render fain unto our better Rome,
Unless our Senate, lest their youth disuse
The war, (but who would?) peace, if begged, refuse.

For now of nothing may our state despair,
Darling of heaven, and of men the care;
Provided that they be what they have been,
Watchful abroad, and honest still within.
For while our Neptune doth a trident shake,
Steeled with those piercing heads, Deane, Monck, and
    Blake   150
And while Jove governs in the highest sphere,
Vainly in hell let Pluto domineer.

The First Anniversary of the Government under His Highness the Lord Protector.

Like the vain curlings of the watery maze,
Which in smooth streams a sinking weight does raise,
So man, declining always, disappears
In the weak circles of increasing years;
And his short tumults of themselves compose,
While flowing time above his head does close.
    Cromwell alone with greater vigour runs,
(Sun-like) the stages of succeeding suns:
And still the day which he doth next restore,
Is the just wonder of the day before.   10
Cromwell alone doth with new lustre spring,
And shines the jewel of the yearly ring.
    'Tis he the force of scattered time contracts,
And in one year the work of ages acts:
While heavy monarchs make a wide return,
Longer, and more malignant than Saturn:
And though they all Platonic years should reign,
In the same posture would be found again.
Their earthy projects under ground they lay,
More slow and brittle than the China clay: 20
Well may they strive to leave them to their son,
For one thing never was by one king done.
Yet some more active for a frontier town,
Took in by proxy, begs a false renown;
Another triumphs at the public cost,
And will have won, if he no more have lost;

They fight by others, but in person wrong,
And only are against their subjects strong;
Their other wars seem but a feigned contest,
This common enemy is still oppressed; 30
If conquerors, on them they turn their might;
If conquered, on them they wreak their spite:
They neither build the temple in their days,
Nor matter for succeeding founders raise;
Nor sacred prophecies consult within,
Much less themselves to perfect them begin;
No other care they bear of things above,
But with astrologers divine and Jove
To know how long their planet yet reprieves
From the deserved fate their guilty lives: 40
Thus (image-like) a useless time they tell,
And with vain sceptre strike the hourly bell,
Nor more contribute to the state of things,
Than wooden heads unto the viol's strings.
 While indefatigable Cromwell hies,
And cuts his way still nearer to the skies,
Learning a music in the region clear,
To tune this lower to that higher sphere.
 So when Amphion did the lute command,
Which the god gave him, with his gentle hand, 50
The rougher stones, unto his measures hewed,
Danced up in order from the quarries rude;
This took a lower, that a higher place,
As he the treble altered, or the bass:
No note he struck, but a new storey was laid,
And the great work ascended while he played.
 The listening structures he with wonder eyed,
And still new stops to various time applied:
Now through the strings a martial rage he throws,
And joining straight the Theban tower arose; 60
Then as he strokes them with a touch more sweet,
The flocking marbles in a palace meet;
But for he most the graver notes did try,
Therefore the temples reared their columns high:
Thus, ere he ceased, his sacred lute creates
Th' harmonious city of the seven gates.
 Such was that wondrous order and consent,

When Cromwell tuned the ruling Instrument,
While tedious statesmen many years did hack,
Framing a liberty that still went back,   70
Whose numerous gorge could swallow in an hour
That island, which the sea cannot devour:
Then our Amphion issues out and sings,
And once he struck, and twice, the powerful strings.

   The Commonwealth then first together came,
And each one entered in the willing frame;
All other matter yields, and may be ruled;
But who the minds of stubborn men can build?
No quarry bears a stone so hardly wrought,
Nor with such labour from its centre brought;   80
None to be sunk in the foundation bends,
Each in the house the highest place contends,
And each the hand that lays him will direct,
And some fall back upon the architect;
Yet all composed by his attractive song,
Into the animated city throng.

   The Commonwealth does through their centres all
Draw the circumference of the public wall;
The crossest spirits here do take their part,
Fastening the contignation which they thwart;   90
And they, whose nature leads them to divide,
Uphold this one, and that the other side;
But the most equal still sustain the height,
And they as pillars keep the work upright,
While the resistance of opposed minds,
The fabric (as with arches) stronger binds,
Which on the basis of a senate free,
Knit by the roof's protecting weight, agree.

   When for his foot he thus a place had found,
He hurls e'er since the world about him round,   100
And in his several aspects, like a star,
Here shines in peace, and thither shoots a war,
While by his beams observing princes steer,
And wisely court the influence they fear.
O would they rather by his pattern won
Kiss the approaching, nor yet angry Son;
And in their numbered footsteps humbly tread
The path where holy oracles do lead;

How might they under such a captain raise
The great designs kept for the latter days! 110
But mad with reason (so miscalled) of state
They know them not, and what they know not, hate.
Hence still they sing hosanna to the whore,
And her, whom they should massacre, adore:
But Indians, whom they should convert, subdue;
Nor teach, but traffic with, or burn the Jew.

   Unhappy princes, ignorantly bred,
By malice some, by error more misled,
If gracious heaven to my life give length,
Leisure to time, and to my weakness strength, 120
Then shall I once with graver accents shake
Your regal sloth, and your long slumbers wake:
Like the shrill huntsman that prevents the east,
Winding his horn to kings that chase the beast.

   Till then my muse shall hollo far behind
Angelic Cromwell who outwings the wind,
And in dark nights, and in cold days alone
Pursues the monster thorough every throne:
Which shrinking to her Roman den impure,
Gnashes her gory teeth; nor there secure. 130

   Hence oft I think if in some happy hour
High grace should meet in one with highest power,
And then a seasonable people still
Should bend to his, as he to heaven's will,
What we might hope, what wonderful effect
From such a wished conjuncture might reflect.
Sure, the mysterious work, where none withstand,
Would forthwith finish under such a hand:
Foreshortened time its useless course would stay,
And soon precipitate the latest day. 140
But a thick cloud about that morning lies,
And intercepts the beams of mortal eyes,
That 'tis the most which we determine can,
If these the times, then this must be the man.
And well he therefore does, and well has guessed,
Who in his age has always forward pressed:
And knowing not where heaven's choice may light,
Girds yet his sword, and ready stands to fight;
But men, alas, as if they nothing cared,

Look on, all unconcerned, or unprepared;   150
And stars still fall, and still the dragon's tail
Swinges the volumes of its horrid flail.
For the great justice that did first suspend
The world by sin, does by the same extend.
Hence that blest day still counterpoised wastes,
The ill delaying what the elected hastes;
Hence landing nature to new seas is tossed,
And good designs still with their authors lost.

    And thou, great Cromwell, for whose happy birth
A mould was chosen out of better earth;   160
Whose saint-like mother we did lately see
Live out an age, long as a pedigree;
That she might seem (could we the Fall dispute),
T'have smelled the blossom, and not eat the fruit;
Though none does of more lasting parents grow,
But never any did them honour so,
Though thou thine heart from evil still unstained,
And always hast thy tongue from fraud refrained;
Thou, who so oft through storms of thundering lead
Hast born securely thine undaunted head,   170
Thy breast through poniarding conspiracies,
Drawn from the sheath of lying prophecies;
Thee proof beyond all other force or skill,
Our sins endanger, and shall one day kill.
How near they failed, and in thy sudden fall
At once assayed to overturn us all.
Our brutish fury struggling to be free,
Hurried thy horses, while they hurried thee,
When thou hadst almost quit thy mortal cares,
And soiled in dust thy crown of silver hairs.   180
Let this one sorrow interweave among
The other glories of our yearly song.
Like skilful looms, which through the costly thread
Of purling ore, a shining wave do shed:
So shall the tears we on past grief employ,
Still as they trickle, glitter in our joy.
So with more modesty we may be true,
And speak, as of the dead, the praises due:
While impious men deceived with pleasure short,
On their own hopes shall find the fall retort.   190

But the poor beasts, wanting their noble guide,
(What could they more?) shrunk guiltily aside.
First winged fear transports them far away,
And leaden sorrow then their flight did stay.
See how they each his towering crest abate,
And the green grass, and their known mangers hate,
Nor through wide nostrils snuff the wanton air,
Nor their round hooves, or curled manes compare;
With wandering eyes, and restless ears they stood,
And with shrill neighings asked him of the wood.   200
Thou, Cromwell, falling, not a stupid tree,
Or rock so savage, but it mourned for thee:
And all about was heard a panic groan,
As if that Nature's self were overthrown.
It seemed the earth did from the centre tear;
It seemed the sun was fallen out of the sphere:
Justice obstructed lay, and reason fooled;
Courage disheartened, and religion cooled.
A dismal silence through the palace went,
And then loud shrieks the vaulted marbles rent,   210
Such as the dying chorus sings by turns,
And to deaf seas, the ruthless tempest mourns,
When now they sink, and now the plundering streams
Break up each deck, and rip the oaken seams.
  But thee triumphant hence the fiery car,
And fiery steeds had borne out of the war,
From the low world, and thankless men above,
Unto the kingdom blest of peace and love:
We only mourned ourselves, in thine ascent,
Whom thou hadst left beneath with mantle rent.   220
  For all delight of life thou then didst lose,
When to command, thou didst thyself depose;
Resigning up thy privacy so dear,
To turn the headstrong people's charioteer;
For to be Cromwell was a greater thing,
Than aught below, or yet above a king:
Therefore thou rather didst thyself depress,
Yielding to rule, because it made thee less.
  For neither didst thou from the first apply
Thy sober spirit unto things too high,   230
But in thine own fields exercised'st long,

A healthful mind within a body strong;
Till at the seventh time thou in the skies,
As a small cloud, like a man's hand, didst rise;
Then did thick mists and winds the air deform,
And down at last thou poured'st the fertile storm,
Which to the thirsty land did plenty bring,
But, though forewarned, o'ertook and wet the king.

What since he did, a higher force him pushed
Still from behind, and it before him rushed,   240
Though undiscerned among the tumult blind,
Who think those high decrees by man designed.
'Twas heaven would not that his power should cease,
But walk still middle betwixt war and peace:
Choosing each stone, and poising every weight,
Trying the measures of the breadth and height;
Here pulling down, and there erecting new,
Founding a firm state by proportions true.

When Gideon so did from the war retreat,
Yet by the conquest of two kings grown great,   250
He on the peace extends a warlike power,
And Israel silent saw him raze the tower;
And how he Succoth's Elders durst suppress,
With thorns and briars of the wilderness.
No king might ever such a force have done;
Yet would not he be Lord, nor yet his son.

Thou with the same strength, and a heart as plain,
Didst (like thine olive) still refuse to reign,
Though why should others all thy labour spoil,
And brambles be anointed with thine oil,   260
Whose climbing flame, without a timely stop,
Had quickly levelled every cedar's top?
Therefore first growing to thyself a law,
Th'ambitious shrubs thou in just time didst awe.

So have I seen at sea, when whirling winds,
Hurry the bark, but more the seamen's minds,
Who with mistaken course salute the sand,
And threatening rocks misapprehend for land,
While baleful Tritons to the shipwreck guide,
And corposants along the tacklings slide,   270
The passengers all wearied out before,
Giddy, and wishing for the fatal shore,

Some lusty mate, who with more careful eye
Counted the hours, and every star did spy,
The helm does from the artless steersman strain,
And doubles back unto the safer main.
What though a while they grumble discontent,
Saving himself, he does their loss prevent.
    'Tis not a freedom, that where all command;
Nor tyranny, where one does them withstand: 280
But who of both the bounders knows to lay
Him as their father must the state obey.
    Thou, and thine house (like Noah's eight) did rest,
Left by the wars' flood on the mountains' crest:
And the large vale lay subject to thy will,
Which thou but as a husbandman wouldst till:
And only didst for others plant the vine
Of liberty, not drunken with its wine.
    That sober liberty which men may have,
That they enjoy, but more they vainly crave: 290
And such as to their parents' tents do press,
May show their own, not see his nakedness.
    Yet such a Chammish issue still does rage,
The shame and plague both of the land and age,
Who watched thy halting, and thy fall deride,
Rejoicing when thy foot had slipped aside,
That their new king might the fifth sceptre shake,
And make the world, by his example, quake:
Whose frantic army should they want for men
Might muster heresies, so one were ten.   300
What thy misfortune, they the spirit call,
And their religion only is to fall.
Oh Mahomet! now couldst thou rise again,
Thy falling-sickness should have made thee reign,
While Feake and Simpson would in many a tome,
Have writ the comments of thy sacred foam:
For soon thou mightst have passed among their rant
Were't but for thine unmoved tulipant;
As thou must needs have owned them of thy band
For prophecies fit to be *Alcoraned*.   310
    Accursed locusts, whom your king does spit
Out of the centre of the unbottomed pit;
Wanderers, adulterers, liars, Munser's rest,

Sorcerers, atheists, Jesuits possessed;
You who the scriptures and the laws deface
With the same liberty as points and lace;
Oh race most hypocritically strict!
Bent to reduce us to the ancient Pict;
Well may you act the Adam and the Eve;
Ay, and the serpent too that did deceive.   320

   But the great captain, now the danger's o'er,
Makes you for his sake tremble one fit more;
And, to your spite, returning yet alive
Does with himself all that is good revive.

   So when first man did through the morning new
See the bright sun his shining race pursue,
All day he followed with unwearied sight,
Pleased with that other world of moving light;
But thought him when he missed his setting beams,
Sunk in the hills, or plunged below the streams.   330
While dismal blacks hung round the universe,
And stars (like tapers) burned upon his hearse:
And owls and ravens with their screeching noise
Did make the funerals sadder by their joys.
His weeping eyes the doleful vigils keep,
Not knowing yet the night was made for sleep:
Still to the west, where he him lost, he turned,
And with such accents as despairing mourned:
'Why did mine eyes once see so bright a ray;
Or why day last no longer than a day?'   340
When straight the sun behind him he descried,
Smiling serenely from the further side.

   So while our star that gives us light and heat,
Seemed now a long and gloomy night to threat,
Up from the other world his flame he darts,
And princes (shining through their windows) starts,
Who their suspected counsellors refuse,
And credulous ambassadors accuse.

   'Is this', saith one, 'the nation that we read
Spent with both wars, under a captain dead,   350
Yet rig a navy while we dress us late,
And ere we dine, raze and rebuild their state?
What oaken forests, and what golden mines!
What mints of men, what union of designs!

(Unless their ships, do, as their fowl proceed
Of shedding leaves, that with their ocean breed).
Theirs are not ships, but rather arks of war
And beaked promontories sailed from far;
Of floating islands a new hatched nest;
A fleet of worlds, of other worlds in quest;   360
A hideous shoal of wood-leviathans,
Armed with three tier of brazen hurricanes,
That through the centre shoot their thundering side
And sink the earth that does at anchor ride.
What refuge to escape them can be found,
Whose watery leaguers all the world surround?
Needs must we all their tributaries be,
Whose navies hold the sluices of the sea.
The ocean is the fountain of command,
But that once took, we captives are on land.   370
And those that have the waters for their share,
Can quickly leave us neither earth nor air.
Yet if through these our fears could find a pass,
Through double oak, and lined with treble brass,
That one man still, although but named, alarms
More than all men, all navies, and all arms.
Him, all the day, him, in late nights I dread,
And still his sword seems hanging o'er my head.
The nation had been ours, but his one soul
Moves the great bulk, and animates the whole.   380
He secrecy with number hath enchased,
Courage with age, maturity with haste:
The valiant's terror, riddle of the wise,
And still his falchion all our knots unties.
Where did he learn those arts that cost us dear?
Where below earth, or where above the sphere?
He seems a king by long succession born,
And yet the same to be a king does scorn.
Abroad a king he seems, and something more,
At home a subject on the equal floor.   390
O could I once him with our title see,
So should I hope that he might die as we.
But let them write his praise that love him best,
It grieves me sore to have thus much confessed.'
   Pardon, great Prince, if thus their fear or spite

More than our love and duty do thee right.
I yield, nor further will the prize contend,
So that we both alike may miss our end:
While thou thy venerable head dost raise
As far above their malice as my praise,   400
And as the angel of our commonweal,
Troubling the waters, yearly mak'st them heal.

On the Victory obtained by Blake over the Spaniards in the Bay of Santa Cruz, in the Island of Tenerife, 1657

Now does Spain's fleet her spacious wings unfold,
Leaves the new world and hastens for the old:
But though the wind was fair, they slowly swum
Freighted with acted guilt, and guilt to come:
For this rich load, of which so proud they are,
Was raised by tyranny, and raised for war;
Every capacious galleon's womb was filled,
With what the womb of wealthy kingdoms yield,
The new world's wounded entrails they had tore,
For wealth wherewith to wound the old once more: 10
Wealth which all others' avarice might cloy,
But yet in them caused as much fear as joy.
For now upon the main, themselves they saw—
That boundless empire, where you give the law—
Of winds' and waters' rage, they fearful be,
But much more fearful are your flags to see.
Day, that to those who sail upon the deep,
More wished for, and more welcome is than sleep,
They dreaded to behold, lest the sun's light,
With English streamers, should salute their sight: 20
In thickest darkness they would choose to steer,
So that such darkness might suppress their fear;
At length theirs vanishes, and fortune smiles;
For they behold the sweet Canary Isles;
One of which doubtless is by nature blessed
Above both worlds, since 'tis above the rest.

For lest some gloominess might strain her sky,
Trees there the duty of the clouds supply;
O noble trust which heaven on this isle pours,
Fertile to be, yet never need her showers.   30
A happy people, which at once do gain
The benefits without the ills of rain.
Both health and profit fate cannot deny;
Where still the earth is moist, the air still dry;
The jarring elements no discord know,
Fuel and rain together kindly grow;
And coolness there, with heat doth never fight,
This only rules by day, and that by night.
    Your worth to all these isles, a just right brings,
The best of lands should have the best of kings.   40
And these want nothing heaven can afford,
Unless it be—the having you their lord;
But this great want will not a long one prove,
Your conquering sword will soon that want remove.
For Spain had better—she'll ere long confess—
Have broken all her swords, than this one peace,
Casting that league off, which she held so long,
She cast off that which only made her strong.
Forces and art, she soon will feel, are vain,
Peace, against you, was the sole strength of Spain.   50
By that alone those islands she secures,
Peace made them hers, but war will make them yours.
There the indulgent soil that rich grape breeds,
Which of the gods the fancied drink exceeds;
They still do yield, such is their precious mould,
All that is good, and are not cursed with gold—
With fatal gold, for still where that does grow,
Neither the soil, not people, quiet know.
Which troubles men to raise it when 'tis ore,
And when 'tis raised, does trouble them much more.   60
Ah, why was thither brought that cause of war,
Kind Nature had from thence removed so far?
In vain doth she those islands free from ill,
If fortune can make guilty what she will.
But whilst I draw that scene, where you ere long,
Shall conquests act, your present are unsung.
    For Santa Cruz the glad fleet takes her way,

And safely there casts anchor in the bay.
Never so many with one joyful cry,
That place saluted, where they all must die.   70
Deluded men! Fate with you did but sport,
You 'scaped the sea, to perish in your port.
'Twas more for England's fame you should die there,
Where you had most of strength, and least of fear.
   The peak's proud height the Spaniards all admire,
Yet in their breasts carry a pride much higher.
Only to this vast hill a power is given,
At once both to inhabit earth and heaven.
But this stupendous prospect did not near,
Make them admire, so much as they did fear.   80
   For here they met with news, which did produce,
A grief, above the cure of grapes' best juice.
They learned with terror that nor summer's heat,
Nor winter's storms, had made your fleet retreat.
To fight against such foes was vain, they knew,
Which did the rage of elements subdue,
Who on the ocean that does horror give,
To all besides, triumphantly do live.
   With haste they therefore all their galleons moor,
And flank with cannon from the neighbouring shore.   90
Forts, lines, and sconces all the bay along,
They build and act all that can make them strong.
   Fond men who know not whilst such works they raise,
They only labour to exalt your praise.
Yet they by restless toil became at length,
So proud and confident of their made strength,
That they with joy their boasting general heard,
Wish then for that assault he lately feared.
His wish he has, for now undaunted Blake,
With winged speed, for Santa Cruz does make.   100
For your renown, his conquering fleet does ride,
O'er seas as vast as in the Spaniards' pride.
Whose fleet and trenches viewed, he soon did say,
'We to their strength are more obliged than they.
Were't not for that, they from their fate would run,
And a third world seek out, our arms to shun.
Those forts, which there so high and strong appear,
Do not so much suppress, as show their fear.

Of speedy victory let no man doubt,
Our worst work's past, now we have found them out.   110
Behold their navy does at anchor lie,
And they are ours, for now they cannot fly.'
    This said, the whole fleet gave it their applause,
And all assumes your courage, in your cause.
That bay they enter, which unto them owes,
The noblest wreaths, that victory bestows.
Bold Stayner leads: this fleet's designed by fate,
To give him laurel, as the last did plate.
    The thundering cannon now begins the fight,
And though it be at noon creates a night.   120
The air was soon after the fight begun,
Far more enflamed by it than by the sun.
Never so burning was that climate known,
War turned the temperate to the torrid zone.
    Fate these two fleets between both worlds had brought,
Who fight, as if for both those worlds they fought.
Thousands of ways thousands of men there die,
Some ships are sunk, some blown up in the sky.
Nature ne'er made cedars so high aspire,
As oaks did then, urged by the active fire,   130
Which by quick powder's force, so high was sent,
That it returned to its own element.
Torn limbs some leagues into the island fly,
Whilst others lower in the sea do lie.
Scarce souls from bodies severed are so far
By death, as bodies there were by the war.
The all-seeing sun, ne'er gazed on such a sight,
Two dreadful navies there at anchor fight.
And neither have or power or will to fly,
There one must conquer, or there both must die.   140
Far different motives yet engaged them thus,
Necessity did them, but choice did us.
    A choice which did the highest worth express,
And was attended by as high success.
For your resistless genius there did reign,
By which we laurels reaped e'en on the main.
So prosperous stars, though absent to the sense,
Bless those they shine for, by their influence.
    Our cannon now tears every ship and sconce,

And o'er two elements triumphs at once.   150
Their galleons sunk, their wealth the sea does fill—
The only place where it can cause no ill.
  Ah, would those treasures which both Indies have,
Were buried in as large, and deep a grave,
Wars' chief support with them would buried be,
And the land owe her peace unto the sea.
Ages to come your conquering arms will bless,
There they destroy what had destroyed their peace.
And in one war the present age may boast
The certain seeds of many wars are lost.   160
  All the foe's ships destroyed, by sea or fire,
Victorious Blake, does from the bay retire,
His siege of Spain he then again pursues,
And there first brings of his success the news:
The saddest news that e'er to Spain was brought,
Their rich fleet sunk, and ours with laurel fraught,
Whilst fame in every place her trumpet blows,
And tells the world how much to you it owes.

Two Songs at the Marriage of the Lord Fauconberg and the Lady Mary Cromwell

FIRST SONG
Chorus Endymion Luna

CHORUS

The astrologer's own eyes are set,
And even wolves the sheep forget;
Only this shepherd, late and soon,
Upon this hill outwakes the moon.
Hark how he sings, with sad delight,
Thorough the clear and silent night.

ENDYMION

Cynthia, O Cynthia, turn thine ear,
Nor scorn Endymion's plaints to hear.
As we our flocks, so you command
The fleecy clouds with silver wand.   10

CYNTHIA

If thou a mortal, rather sleep;
Or if a shepherd, watch thy sheep.

ENDYMION

The shepherd, since he saw thine eyes,
And sheep are both thy sacrifice.
Nor merits he a mortal's name,
That burns with an immortal flame.

CYNTHIA

I have enough for me to do,
Ruling the waves that ebb and flow.

ENDYMION

Since thou disdain'st not then to share
On sublunary things thy care;   20
Rather restrain these double seas,
Mine eyes' uncessant deluges.

CYNTHIA

My wakeful lamp all night must move,
Securing their repose above.

ENDYMION

If therefore thy resplendent ray
Can make a night more bright than day,
Shine thorough this obscurer breast,
With shades of deep despair oppressed.

CHORUS

Courage, Endymion, boldly woo;
Anchises was a shepherd too: 30
Yet is her younger sister laid
Sporting with him in Ida's shade:
  And Cynthia, though the strongest,
Seeks but the honour to have held out longest.

ENDYMION

Here unto Latmos' top I climb:
How far below thine orb sublime?
O why, as well as eyes to see,
Have I not arms that reach to thee?

CYNTHIA

'Tis needless then that I refuse,
Would you but your own reason use.   40

ENDYMION

Though I so high may not pretend,
It is the same so you descend.

CYNTHIA

These stars would say I do them wrong,
Rivals each one for thee too strong.

ENDYMION

The stars are fixed unto their sphere,
And cannot, though they would, come near.
Less loves set off each other's praise,
While stars eclipse by mixing rays.

CYNTHIA

That cave is dark.

ENDYMION

Then none can spy: 50
Or shine thou there and 'tis the sky.

CHORUS

Joy to Endymion,
For he has Cynthia's favour won.
And Jove himself approves
With his serenest influence their loves.
For he did never love to pair
His progeny above the air;
But to be honest, valiant, wise,
Makes mortals matches fit for deities.

SECOND SONG

Hobbinol Phyllis Tomalin

HOBBINOL

Phyllis, Tomalin, away:
Never such a merry day.
For the northern shepherd's son
Has Menalca's daughter won.

PHYLLIS

Stay till I some flowers ha' tied
In a garland for the bride.

TOMALIN

If thou wouldst a garland bring,
Phyllis, you may wait the spring:
They ha' chosen such an hour
When *she* is the only flower.   10

PHYLLIS

Let's not then at least be seen
Without each a sprig of green.

HOBBINOL

Fear not; at Menalca's hall
There is bays enough for all.
He, when young, as we did graze,
But when old, he planted bays.

TOMALIN

Here *she* comes; but with a look
Far more catching than my hook.
'Twas those eyes, I now dare swear,
Led our lambs we knew not where.   20

HOBBINOL

Not our lambs' own fleeces are
Curled so lovely as her hair:
Nor our sheep new washed can be
Half so white or sweet as *she*.

PHYLLIS

He so looks as fit to keep
Somewhat else than silly sheep.

HOBBINOL

Come, let's in some carol new
Pay to love and them their due.

ALL

Joy to that happy pair,
Whose hopes united banish our despair.   30
    What shepherd could for love pretend,
Whilst all the nymphs on Damon's choice attend?
    What shepherdess could hope to wed
    Before Marina's turn were sped?
    Now lesser beauties may take place,
    And meaner virtues come in play;
                While they,
                Looking from high,
                Shall grace
Our flocks and us with a propitious eye.   40
    But what is most, the gentle swain
    No more shall need of love complain;
    But virtue shall be beauty's hire,
And those be equal that have equal fire.
    Marina yields. Who dares be coy?
Or who despair, now Damon does enjoy?
                Joy to that happy pair,
Whose hopes united banish our despair.

A Poem upon the Death of his late Highness
the Lord Protector

That Providence which had so long the care
Of Cromwell's head, and numbered every hair,
Now in itself (the glass where all appears)
Had seen the period of his golden years:
And thenceforth only did attend to trace
What death might least so fair a life deface.
    The people, which what most they fear esteem,
Death when more horrid, so more noble deem,
And blame the last act, like spectators vain,
Unless the prince whom they applaud be slain.   10
Nor fate indeed can well refuse that right
To those that lived in war, to die in fight.
    But long his valour none had left that could
Endanger him, or clemency that would.

And he whom Nature all for peace had made,
But angry heaven unto war had swayed,
And so less useful where he most desired,
For what he least affected was admired,
Deserved yet an end whose every part,
Should speak the wondrous softness of his heart.   20
   To Love and Grief the fatal writ was signed;
(Those nobler weaknesses of human mind,
From which those powers that issued the decree,
Although immortal, found they were not free),
That they, to whom his breast still open lies,
In gentle passions should his death disguise:
And leave succeeding ages cause to mourn,
As long as Grief shall weep, or Love shall burn.
   Staight does a slow and languishing disease
Eliza, Nature's and his darling, seize.   30
Her when an infant, taken with her charms,
He oft would flourish in his mighty arms,
And, lest their force the tender burden wrong,
Slacken the vigour of his muscles strong;
Then to the mother's breast her softly move,
Which while she drained of milk, she filled with love.
But as with riper years her virtue grew,
And every minute adds a lustre new,
When with meridian height her beauty shined,
And thorough that sparkled her fairer mind,   40
When she with smiles serene and words discreet
His hidden soul at every turn could meet;
Then mighty y'ha daily his affection spied,
Doubling that knot which destiny had tied,
While they by sense, not knowing, comprehend
How on each other both their fates depend.
With her each day the pleasing hours he shares,
And at her aspect calms his growing cares;
Or with a grandsire's joy her children sees
Hanging about her neck or at his knees.   50
Hold fast, dear infants, hold them both or none;
This will not stay when once the other's gone.
   A silent fire now wastes those limbs of wax,
And him within his tortured image racks.
So the flower withering which the garden crowned,

The sad root pines in secret under ground.
Each groan he doubled and each sigh he sighed,
Repeated over to the restless night.
No trembling string composed to numbers new,
Answers the touch in notes more sad, more true.   60
She, lest he grieve, hides what she can her pains,
And he to lessen hers his sorrow feigns:
Yet both perceived, yet both concealed their skills,
And so diminishing increased their ills:
That whether by each other's grief they fell,
Or on their own redoubled, none can tell.

And now Eliza's purple locks were shorn,
Where she so long her father's fate had worn:
And frequent lightning to her soul that flies,
Divides the air, and opens all the skies: 70
And now his life, suspended by her breath,
Ran out impetuously to hasting death.
Like polished mirrors, so his steely breast
Had every figure of her woes expressed,
And with the damp of her last gasp obscured,
Had drawn such stains as were not to be cured.
Fate could not either reach with single stroke,
But the dear image fled, the mirror broke.

Who now shall tell us more of mournful swans,
Of halcyons kind, or bleeding pelicans?   80
No downy breast did e'er so gently beat,
Or fan with airy plumes so soft a heat.
For he no duty by his height excused,
Nor, though a prince, to be a man refused:
But rather than in his Eliza's pain
Not love, not grieve, would neither live nor reign:
And in himself so oft immortal tried,
Yet in compassion of another died.

So have I seen a vine, whose lasting age
Of many a winter hath survived the rage,   90
Under whose shady tent men every year
At its rich blood's expense their sorrow cheer,
If some dear branch where it extends its life
Chance to be pruned by an untimely knife,
The parent tree unto the grief succeeds,
And through the wound its vital humour bleeds,

Trickling in watery drops, whose flowing shape
Weeps that it falls ere fixed into a grape.
So the dry stock, no more that spreading vine,
Frustrates the autumn and the hopes of wine.   100
  A secret cause does sure those signs ordain
Foreboding princes' falls, and seldom vain.
Whether some kinder powers that wish us well,
What they above cannot prevent foretell;
Or the great world do by consent presage,
As hollow seas with future tempests rage;
Or rather heaven, which us so long forsees,
Their funerals celebrates while it decrees.
But never yet was any human fate
By Nature solemnized with so much state.   110
He unconcerned the dreadful passage crossed;
But, oh, what pangs that death did Nature cost!
First the great thunder was shot off, and sent
The signal from the starry battlement.
The winds receive it, and its force outdo,
As practising how they could thunder too;
Out of the binder's hand the sheaves they tore,
And thrashed the harvest in the airy floor;
Or of huge trees, whose growth with his did rise,
The deep foundations opened to the skies.   120
Then heavy showers the winged tempests lead,
And pour the deluge o'er the chaos' head.
The race of warlike horses at his tomb
Offer themselves in many a hetacomb;
With pensive head towards the ground they fall,
And helpless languish at the tainted stall.
Numbers of men decrease with pains unknown,
And hasten, not to see his death, their own.
Such tortures all the elements unfixed,
Troubled to part where so exactly mixed.   130
And as through air his wasting spirits flowed,
The universe laboured beneath their load.
  Nature, it seemed with him would Nature vie;
He with Eliza, it with him would die.
  He without noise still travelled to his end,
As silent suns to meet the night descend.
The stars that for him fought had only power

Left to determine now his fatal hour,
Which, since they might not hinder, yet they cast
To choose it worthy of his glories past.   140
    No part of time but bare his mark away
Of honour; all the year was Cromwell's day:
But this, of all the most auspicious found,
Twice had in open field him victor crowned:
When up the armed mountains of Dunbar
He marched, and through deep Severn ending war.
What day should him externize but the same
That had before immortalized his name?
That so who ere would at his death have joyed,
In their own griefs might find themselves employed;   150
But those that sadly his departure grieved,
Yet joyed, remembering what he once achieved.
And the last minute his victorious ghost
Gave chase to Ligny on the Belgic coast.
Here ended all his mortal toils: he laid
And slept in peace under the laurel shade.
    O Cromwell, heaven's favourite! To none
Have such high honours from above been shown:
For whom the elements we mourners see,
And heaven itself would the great herald be,   160
Which with more care set forth his obsequies
Than those of Moses hid from human eyes,
As jealous only here lest all be less,
That we could to his memory express.
    Then let us to our course of mourning keep:
Where heaven leads, 'tis piety to weep.
Stand back, ye seas, and shrunk beneath the veil
Of your abyss, with covered head bewail
Your monarch: we demand not your supplies
To compass in our isle; our tears suffice: 170
Since him away the dismal tempest rent,
Who once more joined us to the continent;
Who planted England on the Flandric shore,
And stretched our frontier to the Indian ore;
Whose greater truths obscure the fables old,
Whether of British saints or worthies told;
And in a valour lessening Arthur's deeds,
For holiness the Confessor exceeds.

He first put arms into Religion's hand,
And timorous Conscience unto Courage manned: 180
The soldier taught that inward mail to wear,
And fearing God how they should nothing fear.
'Those strokes', he said, 'will pierce through all below
Where those that strike from heaven fetch their blow.'
Astonished armies did their flight prepare,
And cities strong were stormed by his prayer;
Of that, forever Preston's field shall tell
The story, and impregnable Clonmel.
And where the sandy mountain Fenwick scaled,
The sea between, yet hence his prayer prevailed.   190
What man was ever so in heaven obeyed
Since the commanded sun o'er Gibeon stayed?
In all his wars needs must he triumph when
He conquered God still ere he fought with men.

   Hence, though in battle none so brave or fierce,
Yet him the adverse steel could never pierce.
Pity it seemed to hurt him more that felt
Each wound himself which he to others dealt;
Danger itself refusing to offend
So loose an enemy, so fast a friend.   200

   Friendship, that sacred virtue, long does claim
The first foundation of his house and name:
But within one its narrow limits fall,
His tenderness extended unto all.
And that deep soul through every channel flows,
Where kindly nature loves itself to lose.
More strong affections never reason served,
Yet still affected most what best deserved.
If he Eliza loved to that degree,
(Though who more worthy to be loved than she?)   210
If so indulgent to his own, how dear
To him the children of the highest were?
For her he once did nature's tribute pay:
For these his life adventured every day:
And 'twould be found, could we his thoughts have cast,
Their griefs struck deepest, if Eliza's last.
What prudence more than human did he need
To keep so dear, so differing minds agreed?
The worser sort, as conscious of their ill,

Lie weak and easy to the ruler's will;   220
But to the good (too many or too few)
All law is useless, all reward is due.
Oh ill-advised, if not for love, for shame,
Spare yet your own, if you neglect his fame;
Lest others dare to think your zeal a mask,
And you to govern, only heaven's task.
Valour, religion, friendship, prudence died
At once with him, and all that's good beside;
And we death's refuse, nature's dregs, confined
To loathsome life, alas! are left behind.   230
Where we (so once we used) shall now no more
To fetch day, press about his chamber door—
From which he issued with that awful state,
It seemed Mars broke through Janus' double gate,
Yet always tempered with an air so mild,
No April suns that e'er so gently smiled—
No more shall hear that powerful language charm,
Whose force oft spared the labour of his arm:
No more shall follow where he spent the days
In war, in counsel, or in prayer and praise,   240
Whose meanest acts he would himself advance,
As ungirt David to the ark did dance.
All, all is gone of ours or his delight
In horses fierce, wild deer, or armour bright;
Francisca fair can nothing now but weep,
Nor with soft notes shall sing his cares asleep.
    I saw him dead. A leaden slumber lies
And mortal sleep over those wakeful eyes:
Those gentle rays under the lids were fled,
Which through his looks that piercing sweetness shed;   250
That port which so majestic was and strong,
Loose and deprived of vigour, stretched along:
All withered, all discoloured, pale and wan—
How much another thing, nor more that man?
Oh human glory vain, oh death, oh wings,
Oh worthless world, oh transitory things!
Yet dwelt that greatness in his shape decayed,
That still though dead, greater than death he laid;
And in his altered face you something feign
That threatens death he yet will live again.   260

Not much unlike the sacred oak which shoots
To heaven its branches and through earth its roots,
Whose spacious boughs are hung with trophies round,
And honoured wreaths have oft the victor crowned.
When angry Jove darts lightning through the air,
At mortals' sins, nor his own plant will spare,
(It groans, and bruises all below, that stood
So many years the shelter of the wood.)
The tree erewhile foreshortened to our view,
When fallen shows taller yet than as it grew: 270
So shall his praise to after times increase,
When truth shall be allowed, and faction cease,
And his own shadows with him fall. The eye
Detracts from objects than itself more high:
But when death takes them from that envied seat,
Seeing how little, we confess how great.
Thee, many ages hence in martial verse
Shall the English soldier, ere he charge, rehearse,
Singing of thee, inflame themselves to fight,
And with the name of Cromwell, armies fright.   280
As long as rivers to the seas shall run,
As long as Cynthia shall relieve the sun,
While stags shall fly unto the forests thick,
While sheep delight the grassy downs to pick,
As long as future time succeeds the past,
Always thy honour, praise, and name shall last.

   Thou in a pitch how far beyond the sphere
Of human glory towerst, and reigning there
Despoiled of mortal robes, in seas of bliss,
Plunging dost bathe, and tread the bright abyss: 290
There thy great soul at once a world does see,
Spacious enough, and pure enough for thee.
How soon thou Moses hast, and Joshua found,
And David for the sword and harp renowned?
How straight canst to each happy mansion go?
(Far better known above than here below)
And in those joys dost spend the endless day,
Which in expressing we ourselves betray.

   For we, since thou art gone, with heavy doom,
Wander like ghosts about thy loved tomb;   300
And lost in tears, have neither sight nor mind

To guide us upward through this region blind.
Since thou art gone, who best that way couldst teach,
Only our sighs, perhaps, may thither reach.

And Richard yet, where his great parent led,
Beats on the rugged track: he, virtue dead,
Revives, and by his milder beams assures;
And yet how much of them his grief obscures?

He, as his father, long was kept from sight
In private, to be viewed by better light;   310
But opened once, what splendour does he throw?
A Cromwell in an hour a prince will grow.
How he becomes that seat, how strongly strains,
How gently winds at once the ruling reins?
Heaven to this choice prepared a diadem,
Richer than any Eastern silk or gem;
A pearly rainbow, where the sun enchased
His brows, like an imperial jewel graced.

We find already what those omens mean,
Earth ne'er more glad, nor heaven more serene.   320
Cease now our griefs, calm peace succeeds a war,
Rainbows to storms, Richard to Oliver.
Tempt not his clemency to try his power,
He threats no deluge, yet foretells a shower.

On Mr Milton's 'Paradise Lost'

When I beheld the poet blind, yet bold,
In slender book his vast design unfold,
Messiah crowned, God's reconciled decree,
Rebelling angels, the Forbidden Tree,
Heaven, hell, earth, chaos, all; the argument
Held me a while, misdoubting his intent
That he would ruin (for I saw him strong)
The sacred truths to fable and old song,
(So Samson groped the temple's posts in spite)
The world o'erwhelming to revenge his sight.   10

Yet as I read, soon growing less severe,
I liked his project, the success did fear;
Through that wide field how he his way should find

O'er which lame faith leads understanding blind;
Lest he perplexed the things he would explain,
And what was easy he should render vain.

Or if a work so infinite he spanned,
Jealous I was that some less skilful hand
(Such as disquiet always what is well,
And by ill imitating would excel) 20
Might hence presume the whole creation's day
To change in scenes, and show it in a play.

Pardon me, mighty poet, nor despise
My causeless, yet not impious, surmise.
But I am now convinced that none will dare
Within thy labours to pretend a share.
Thou hast not missed one thought that could be fit,
And all that was improper dost omit:
So that no room is here for writers left,
But to detect their ignorance or theft. 30

That majesty which through thy work doth reign
Draws the devout, deterring the profane.
And things divine thou treat'st of in such state
As them preserves, and thee, inviolate.
At once delight and horror on us seize,
Thou sing'st with so much gravity and ease;
And above human flight dost soar aloft,
With plume so strong, so equal, and so soft.
The bird named from that paradise you sing
So never flags, but always keeps on wing. 40

Where couldst thou words of such a compass find?
Whence furnish such a vast expense of mind?
Just heaven thee, like Tiresias, to requite,
Rewards with prophecy thy loss of sight.

Well mightst thou scorn thy readers to allure
With tinkling rhyme, of thy own sense secure;
While the *Town-Bays* writes all the while and spells,
And like a pack-horse tires without his bells.
Their fancies like our bushy points appear,
The poets tag them; we for fashion wear. 50
I too, transported by the mode, offend,
And while I meant to *praise* thee must commend.
Thy verse created like thy theme sublime,
In number, weight, and measure, needs not rhyme.

Notes

ABBREVIATIONS

1681   *Miscellaneous Poems*. By Andrew Marvell. 1681. (The British
                 Library copy, C.59.i.8.)

Bodleian MS   Bodleian MS. Eng. poet. d. 49. (A copy of *1681* with
                 manuscript corrections and additions.)

Cooke   *The Works of Andrew Marvell*, ed. Thomas Cooke (2 vols.,
                 1726).

Donno   *Andrew Marvell: The Complete Poems*, ed. Elizabeth Story
                 Donno (1972).

Grosart   *The Complete Works of Andrew Marvell*, ed. A. B. Grosart (4
                 vols., 1872–5).

Kermode   *The Selected Poetry of Marvell*, ed. Frank Kermode (New
                 York, 1967).

Lord   *Andrew Marvell: Complete Poetry*, ed. George de F. Lord
                 (New York, 1968; London, 1984).

Margoliouth   *The Poems and Letters of Andrew Marvell*, ed. H. M. Margoli-
                 outh (2 vols., Oxford, 1927); 3rd edn. revised by Pierre
                 Legouis and E. E. Duncan-Jones (2 vols., Oxford, 1971).

Smith   *'The Rehearsal Transpros'd' and 'The Rehearsal Transpros'd
                 The Second Part'*, ed. D. I. B. Smith (Oxford, 1971).

Thompson   *The Works of Andrew Marvell*, ed. Edward Thompson (3
                 vols., 1776).

Wilcher   *Andrew Marvell: Selected Poetry and Prose*, ed. Robert Wilcher
                 (1986).

Other works abbreviated will be found under 'Further Reading' (p. 170),
or in the headnotes to individual poems.

  1 *An Elegy upon the Death of my Lord Francis Villiers*. Surviving in an
    apparently unique quarto from the library of Sir George Clarke
    (1661–1736), now in the library of Worcester College, Oxford. The
    poem is ascribed to Marvell by Clarke (for details see Margoliouth).
    The attribution has not gone unchallenged.
      Francis Villiers (b. 1629), second and posthumous son of George,
    first Duke of Buckingham, was killed 7 July 1648, at a skirmish near
    Kingston. (See S. R. Gardiner, *History of the Great Civil War*, 4, 160.)

l. 18. *bloody bays*: Rosemary dipped in blood was placed upon the coffins of soldiers (Duncan-Jones).

l. 30. *his princess*: Lady Katherine Manners, Duchess of Buckingham.

ll. 31–2. *As the wise Chinese . . . entomb*: cf. 'The First Anniversary', ll. 19–20.

l. 40. *acceptably*: stressed on the first and third syllables.

l. 41. *'Tis truth . . . dispraise*: cf. Eccles. 11:2: 'Commend not a man for his beauty' (Duncan-Jones).

2 l. 61. *Fair Richmond*: Mary Villiers married James Stuart, first Duke of Richmond.

l. 69. *Clora*: probably Mary Kirke, daughter of the poet Aurelian Townsend.

l. 81. *modest plant: mimosa pudica* or sensitive plant.

l. 84. *feign*: dissemble or conceal.

3 ll. 98–100. *The Sad Iliads . . . would spare*: cf. *Aeneid*, iv. 186–7.

l. 123. *own*: due.

4 *To his Noble Friend Mr Richard Lovelace, upon his Poems.* A commendatory poem prefixed to Lovelace's *Lucasta* (1649).

l. 2. *with*: proposed by R. G. Howarth, *Notes and Queries*, 198 (1953), 380; 'which' *1649*.

l. 5. *could tell*: knew.

l. 12. *civic crown*: an oak-leaf garland bestowed on one who saves a citizen's life in battle.

l. 20. *Of wit . . . sons*: born ill-shaped of the corruption of wit, as insects of rotten matter.

ll. 21–2. *censurers . . . book*: in June 1643 Parliament issued an Ordinance against the printing of unlicensed books and this remained in force (despite *Areopagitica*, 1644, and other protests). *Lucasta* was licensed in 1648.   *consistory*. Court of presbyters.

l. 24. *young presbytery*: established in 1643.

l. 28. *wronged*: abused.   *the House's privilege*: parliamentary privilege includes immunity from action in the courts for what is said in the House. In *Lucasta*, that is, Lovelace assumed a freedom of speech granted only to Members in the House.

l. 29. *sequestrian*: Lovelace's estate was ordered to be confiscated on 28 Nov. 1648.

l. 30. *Because . . . war*: referring to Lovelace's song 'To Lucasta going to the wars'.

ll. 31-2. *Kent . . . sent*: Lovelace was sent to prison for presenting to the House of Commons (April 1642) a Kentish petition asking for control of the militia and the use of the Book of Common Prayer.

5 *Upon the death of Lord Hastings.* First published in *Lachrymae Musarum* (1649), a collection of funeral elegies for Henry Lord Hastings, who died of smallpox on 24 June. The funeral elegy was a genre requiring a high conceited style. Contributors to the collection included Herrick, Denham, and the 18-year-old Dryden.

l. 11. *phlegmatic*: accented on the first syllable.

l. 12. *remora*: the sucking-fish, believed by the ancients to have the power of staying the course of any ship to which it attached itself.

ll. 13-16. *What man . . . already old*: some live to attain a second childhood; others develop so fast that while still young they are treated as if they were old, and die prematurely.

l. 18. *But . . . geometric year*: The contrast may be between arithmetical numbering and geometrical proportion, the former sequential, the latter accounting not for numbers but ratios (so that maturity, early or late, qualifies for death). E. E. Duncan-Jones finds an explanation in J. Wilkins, *Mathematical Magic* (1648), which refers to an artificial motion geometrically contrived to be swifter than the revolution of the heavens. A 'geometric year' would be one that passes more quickly.

l. 23. *that state*: heaven.

l. 24. *more than one*: both the trees.

ll. 25-6. *Therefore . . . ostracize*: the astrological conjunction which brought about his death acted like democracy—it excluded someone of worth (i.e. an aristocrat).

6 l. 34. *carousels*: knightly tournaments.

l. 43. *Hymeneus*: the god of marriage, traditionally clothed in a saffron robe and carrying a torch, now wears purple for mourning.

l. 46. *Reversed*: on the analogy of reversed arms at state funerals.

l. 47. *Aesculapius*: god of medicine.

l. 48. *Mayern*: physician to the king, and Hastings' prospective father-in-law.

l. 50. *leap*: explode (*OED*, s.v. 5b).

ll. 53-4. *laurels . . . balsam*: poetry and medicine.

l. 60. *art . . . short*: attributed to Hippocrates, Greek physician.

POEMS PUBLISHED IN *MISCELLANEOUS POEMS*, 1681

7 *A Dialogue, between the Resolved Soul and Created Pleasure.* Mary Palmer or her friends set this poem at the head of *1681*. It could well have

been written as a brief cantata. The scheme of the poem—the rejection of each sense, progressing upwards, and then of the temptations of sex, wealth, and forbidden knowledge—is the scheme used in the temptation of Christ in *Paradise Regained* (1671), book 4.

Resolved: resolute, free from doubt and uncertainty; perhaps with a pun on the musical sense—(having) passed from discord to concord.

ll. 2–4. *shield . . . helmet . . . sword:* Eph. 6: 11, 13, 16, 17: 'Put on the whole armour of God, that ye may be able to stand against the wiles of the devil . . . Wherefore take unto you the whole armour of God, that ye may be able to withstand in the evil day, and having done all, to stand . . . Above all, taking the shield of faith . . . and take the helmet of salvation, and the sword of the Spirit, which is the word of God.' The traditional equipment of the *miles Christi.*

ll. 5–6. *army . . . banners:* S. of S. 6: 4, 10.

ll. 15–16. *Where . . . yours:* where the essences of fruits and flowers will be ready to stimulate your (lower or sensitive) soul.

l. 18. *bait:* take refreshment during a pause on a journey.

l. 21. *plain:* flat or evenly.

l. 22. *Lest one leaf . . . strain.* This line refers to the legend of the Sybarite king Mindyrides whose comfort was impaired by resting on crumpled rose-petals. Seneca, *de Ira*, II. XXV. 2.

8 l. 34. *crystal:* looking-glass.

l. 36. *but:* only.

l. 39. *posting:* hastening.

l. 44. *chordage:* puns on 'cordage' and 'chord' in its sense of 'concord'.

ll. 45–8. *Earth . . . delight:* cf. Seneca, *Ecce spectaculum dignum ad quod respiciat Deus . . . vir fortis cum mala fortuna compositus* (L. N. Wall, *Notes and Queries* (1961), 185–6).   *fence:* ward off.

9 l. 53. *within one beauty.* The painter Zeuxis, believing that in nature all possible beauties could not be found in one body (*uno in corpore:* Cicero, *de Inventione*, ii), used many models for his portrait of Helen. The theme was often moralized. Cf. Cowley, 'The Soul'.

l. 69. *each hidden cause:* the origins of natural phenomena.

l. 71. *centre:* of the earth.

l. 73. *degree:* (1) scale; (2) ladder (with pun on academic sense).

10 l. 76. *not . . . more:* cf. Luke 4: 13, when Jesus has overcome *all* the temptations.

On a Drop of Dew. Marvell wrote a Latin version entitled 'Ros' ('dew'). It is not known which came first.

l. 1. *orient:* sparkling as a pearl. ('Orient' pearls came from the Indian ocean and had more lustre than the European variety.)

l. 3. *blowing:* blossoming.

l. 5. *For:* because of.

l. 6. *encloses:* closes in (intransitive), or '[it] encloses in itself . . .'.

l. 8. *as:* so far as.   *native element:* the heavens.

l. 19. *So the soul:* the association between manna, dew, and grace is ancient, as is the notion that each soul is a small part of the divine.

l. 23. *swart:* Dark (conjectured by Sparrow); 'sweat' *1681*, Margoliouth.

l. 24. *recollecting:* collecting again; remembering.

l. 26. *heaven less:* a lesser heaven.

l. 27. *coy:* modest.

l. 29. *the world excluding round:* thus shutting out the world on every side.

11 l. 34. *girt:* prepared for action.

l. 39. *dissolving:* Exod. 16: 21.

The Coronet

l. 7. *towers:* women's tall head-dresses.

l. 11. *chaplet:* coronet.

l. 14. *twining in:* entwining.

l. 16. *wreaths:* coils.

l. 19. *thou:* Christ.

l. 22. *curious:* elaborately wrought.   *frame:* structure (the chaplet).

l. 26. *feet:* when the serpent's head is bruised by Christ, he will, in the process, destroy the carefully made, but worthless, poems offered him by the penitent; thus what could not serve to crown his head will, accidentally, crown his feet.

12 *Eyes and Tears.* There was a contemporary vogue for conceited poems about tears, especially those of Mary Magdalene; cf. Crashaw, 'The Weeper'. Cf. also Shakespeare, *Venus and Adonis*, ll. 962–3.

l. 3. *That . . . vain:* cf. Eccles. 1: 14.

ll. 5–6. *the . . . height:* the sight, being liable to self-induced error, makes wrong estimates of height by misjudging angles.

ll. 21–4. *So . . . pours:* the sun, like an alchemist, extracts each day the essence of the world, but it turns out to be moisture, which is then poured back.

13 ll. 29–32. *So Magdalen . . . feet: 1681* prints a Latin version of this stanza.

l. 29. *So Magdalen . . . wise:* see Luke 7: 37–8.

l. 35. *Cynthia teeming:* full moon.

14 l. 55. *each . . . bears:* the characteristics of each are transferred to the other.

Bermudas. John Oxenbridge, in whose house at Eton Marvell lived in 1653, had twice been to the Bermudas, first in 1635 as a result of the ecclesiastical persecutions. The islands, thus associated with Puritan exile, had for long been celebrated as a kind of earthly paradise, and the traditional attributes of that place associated with them. They were sometimes known as the Somers Islands, in memory of the captain whose wreck there gave rise to pamphlets on which Shakespeare drew in *The Tempest.* These already suggest that the islands were a paradise, with continual spring and summer together, rich in natural resources and reserved for the godly English. All the traditional lore of the earthly paradise became attached to the Indies, especially Bermuda.

l. 1. *ride:* like a ship at anchor.

l. 7. *so long unknown:* the islands were discovered by Juan Bermudez in 1515.

ll. 9–16. *Where he . . . the air:* as in the *Benedicite,* the whales precede the fowls (Craze, 269).

l. 9. *sea-monsters:* Waller had written of a battle between Bermudans and stranded whales.

l. 15. *fowls:* as the ravens were sent to succour Elijah (1 Kgs. 17: 6), William Strachey, in his *True Repertory of the Wreck* (1610), published in *Purchas's Pilgrims* (1625), describes at length how one easily caught a kind of bird something like a plover and 'fat and full as a partridge'.

l. 20. *Ormus:* Hormuz on the Gulf of Iran.

ll. 21–2. *He makes . . . our feet:* cf. 'The Garden', stanza 5.

l. 23. *apples plants:* i.e. plants apples.

l. 28. *Proclaim:* make manifest.   *ambergris:* fragrant substance excreted by sperm whales.

15 ll. 35–6. *Which thence . . . Mexique Bay:* cf. 'First Anniversary', ll. 345–72 and l. 381   *Beyond . . . Bay:* in order presumably, to convert the heathen and the papist in South America.

ll. 37–40. *Thus sung . . . time:* The 'story of Richard More's party landing in Bermuda in 1612 contains the description of men rowing and the singing of a Psalm of thankfulness' (Margoliouth, quoting Douglas Bush).

Clorinda and Damon

l. 3. *scutcheon:* heraldic arms.

l. 4. *Flora:* goddess of flowers.

l. 7. *Grass . . . fade:* Isa. 40: 8.

l. 8. *vade:* pass away, decay.

l. 9. *cave:* perhaps recalling the cave (*spelunca*) which Dido entered with Aeneas (*Aeneid*, iv. 124).

l. 10. *den:* Stanyhurst (1582) translates *spelunca* by 'den'.

l. 20. *Pan:* Christ, as often in pastoral poetry.

16 l. 23. *oat:* Flute.

A Dialogue between the Soul and Body. A note in the annotated Bodleian copy (Bodleian MS), '*Desunt multa*' (much is missing), suggests this poem is incomplete. The second speech of the Body has four extra lines, which may have survived from a third rejoinder to the Soul. (In the Bodleian MS the lines are scored through.)

The debate between soul and body is a form with a long history, and seems at this time to have had a minor revival. The conflicts and paradoxes of the debate are inherent in Gal. 5: 17: 'For the flesh lusteth against the spirit, and the spirit against the flesh: and these are contrary the one to the other.' K. S. Datta, 'New Light on Marvell's "A Dialogue . . .'", *Renaissance Quarterly*, 22 (1969), stresses the relation between Marvell's poem and an emblem in Hermann Hugo's *Pia Desideria* (1624), citing relevant passages in Plutarch's *Moralia*. She mentions as a notable predecessor Francis Davison's 'A Dialogue between the Soul and Body' in *Poetical Rhapsody* (1602–21).

ll. 1–10. *O, who shall . . . double heart:* borrowed from Hermann Hugo's emblem book *Pia Desideria* (1624), as in '*Pes compes, manicaeque manus, nervique catenae/Ossaque cancellis nexa catasta suis*' ('feet fetters, hands manacles, nerves chains, bones a cage for showing off a slave in the market, bound together with its own lattice-work of bars').

ll. 3–4. *bolts . . . hands:* the violent antithesis between the function of the various organs from the point of view of soul and body is expressed by an assonance, alliterations delayed and given point by the line-ending, and finally by an exploitation of the Latin root (*manus:* hand) of the verb, which represents hand as fetters. This prepares for the flatter paradox concerning the eye, and for the further paradox (reinforced by onomatopoeia) concerning the ear.

l. 10. *vain . . . heart:* so far, the organs have been literally treated, as the physical agents of the soul's imprisonment. A characteristic swerve of wit now uses *head* and *heart* ambiguously; they are still parts of the anatomy for the soul's prison, but carry also the figurative senses of egotism and treachery.

ll. 11–12. *O, who shall . . . tyrannic soul:* cf. Rom. 7: 24.

l. 13. *impales:* the Body is also a prisoner, held erect and penetrated by the animal function of the Soul, given a life that is a mere preparation for death, and as if possessed by a demon.

l. 14. *precipice:* cf. 'after he [Marvell's antagonist Parker] was stretched to such a height in his own fancy, that he could not look down from top to toe but that his eyes dazzled to the precipice of his stature', *Rehearsal Transprosed*, i (1672), 64. Marvell enjoyed the word; see 'Appleton House', l. 375.

l. 15. *needless:* unnecessary; or, having no need of it.

l. 16. *A fever:* perhaps a reminiscence of Donne's 'A Fever'; the disease stimulating the corrupt flow of animal spirits.

17 l. 21. *magic:* referring to the common magical torment of enclosing familiar spirits in trees.

ll. 23–4. *whatsoever . . . pain:* 'it' is the body. Whatever complaint *it* has, *I* experience the pain of, although (except in so far as I animate a body) I am immaterial and so impervious to pain.

ll. 25–6. *all . . . destroys:* I am obliged to devote myself to the preservation of a body whose health is directly opposed to my interests.

l. 29. *the port:* death.

l. 30. *shipwrecked:* the paradox of the happy shipwreck is employed in Shakespeare's *The Tempest* and its sources; also by Crashaw in a Latin epigram *'Ad Bethesdae piscinam positus'* which Marvell probably knew.

l. 32. *maladies:* here spiritual ills are rendered in physical terms, as befits the body.

ll. 43–4. *So . . . grew:* the emphasis is on the perversity of the soul in altering what was natural (indifferent to sin) into something which could, like a building, be occupied by it.

The Nymph complaining for the Death of her Fawn. Poems on the death of a pet have a long history (see e.g. Ovid's poem on Corinna's parrot, *Amores*, ii. 6, and Catullus's on Lesbia's sparrow, 2), and were common in European poetry of this period including English poetry. A fawn is lamented in *Aeneid*, VII. 475 ff.—the lament starts a war— and a hind in the *Punica* of Silius Italicus (13), where the wanton killing again gives rise to conflict. A stag is mourned in Ovid, *Metamorphoses*, x. 106.

l. 1. *troopers:* the word came into use about 1640, and was first applied to soldiers in the Covenanting army, but soon became associated with Cromwell's men.

18 l. 13. *so:* forgotten, unavenged by heaven.

l. 17. *deodands:* any chattel that caused the death of a man was forfeit under law to the king of pious uses; the nymph is saying that if men do not kill beasts with justice, this rule ought to apply equally to them. They would thus be deodands.

ll. 23–4. *There is . . . sin:* the troopers have killed the only thing that could have redeemed the sin they committed in doing so.

ll. 32–6. *dear . . . heart:* these very old pastoral puns are here used as a contribution to the sophisticated naïveté of the tone.

19 l. 70. *four:* disyllabic, as in 'Appleton House', l. 323.

ll. 71–92: *I have a garden . . . roses within:* cf. S. of S. 2: 8–9, 16–17; 5: 1, 10, 13, 16; 6: 2–3; 3: 1. Like the Song of Solomon, 'The Nymph complaining' lacks continuous or systematic allegory, but lends itself to shifting meanings in an allegorical field.

20 l. 97. *balsam:* applied both to the balsam-tree and its resin.

ll. 99–100. *Heliades . . . tears:* the three daughters of Helios, sisters of Phaeton, after mourning their brother's death, were turned into amber-dropping trees. Ovid, *Metamorphoses*, ii. 364–5.

l. 104. *Diana's shrine:* Diana was goddess of both chastity and hunting.

l. 106. *turtles:* doves.

l. 116. *stone:* the nymph imagines her fate as parallel to that of Niobe who, lamenting the death of all her children, was turned to stone. *Metamorphoses*, VI. 146–317.

l. 119. *There: 1681*; 'Then' conjectured by E. E. Duncan-Jones.

Young Love

21 l. 6. *beguiled:* (1) charmed; and (2) deceived.

l. 9. *stay:* wait (till they are fifteen).

l. 11. *green:* immature.

l. 21. *of:* over.

l. 23. *antedate:* anticipate.

22 *To his coy Mistress.* This poem draws upon ancient lyric traditions— the persuasion of a young woman to 'seize the day', the *blason* or catalogue of charms, etc., though the irony and force of the lover's arguments are highly original. The structure of the poem has often been compared to a syllogism: for a comment on its logic see R. I. V. Hodge, *Foreshortened Time* (Cambridge, 1978), 22–4.

l. 8. *ten years before the flood:* i.e. quite near the beginning of time.

l. 10. *conversion of the Jews:* this was expected during the Last Days, near the end of time.

ll. 13–18. *A hundred . . . heart:* the hyperbole derives from the old *blason*, or catalogue of a mistress's beauties, and is anticipated by Cowley in 'My Diet', *The Mistress* (1647), stanza 3:

> On a sigh of pity I a year can live,
>   One tear will keep me twenty at least,
>   Fifty a gentle look will give,
> A hundred years on one kind word I'll feast:
>   A thousand more will added be,
> If you an inclination have for me;
> And all beyond is vast eternity.

l. 22. *Time's . . . chariot:* time is often represented as winged, and often has a chariot; but the conflation appears to be Marvell's own.

ll. 25–9. *Thy beauty . . . dust:* the theme is as old as *The Greek Anthology:* 'You would keep your virginity? What will it profit you? It is among the living that we taste the joys of Venus. You will find no lover in Hades, girl. In Acheron, child, we shall only be bones and dust.' Asklepiades, tr. Forrest Reid, *Poems from the Greek Anthology* (1943), 23.

l. 29. *quaint honour:* while this is perfectly intelligible as a figurative expression, abstract for concrete, Marvell is punning on other than the more common senses of the words, each of which is, in the English of the time, used concretely to mean the female pudenda.

ll. 33–4. *youthful hue . . . morning dew:* Margoliouth; 'youthful hue . . . morning glue (glew)' *1681*; 'youthful glue (glew) . . . morning dew' Bodleian MS. The equivalent couplet in Bodleian MS Don. b. 8 reads:

> Now then whil'st ye youthfull Glue
> Stickes on your Cheeke, like Morning Dew.

The reading 'glue' or 'glew' is attractive, however. As Wilcher says, from its presence in the three earliest texts (the Haward MS [Bodleian Don. b. 8], *1681*, and the Bodleian MS [Eng. Poet. d. 49]), it looks as if the word 'glue' figured in Marvell's poem at some stage of its composition. In Shakespearian English, 'hue' means not only 'colour' but 'appearance' and 'complexion'. *OED* gives an example from 1653.

ll. 35–6. *willing . . . fires:* despite her professed coyness, her amorous spirit shows in her flushed face; it breathes through every pore. Donne uses the same idea in a different context when he says of Elizabeth Drury that 'her pure and eloquent blood | Spoke in her cheeks' ('The Second Anniversary', ll. 244–5).

23 l. 40. *slow-chapped power:* the power of his slowly devouring jaws (*sub . . . lentis maxillis*, Suetonius, *Tiberius*, 21).

ll. 41–6. *Let . . . run.* There has been much discussion of the significance of these images. They are certainly discontinuous, and perhaps derive urgency from that. Margoliouth thinks that in l. 42 Marvell is thinking of a pomander, and in l. 44, 'where the sexual strife is waged', the 'gates of life' suggest the narrow reach known as the Iron Gate, which separates the upper from the lower Danube. Or: Alexander was supposed to have built vast gates to hold back the Scythians—the tribes of Gog and Magog— behind the Urals; at the coming of Antichrist these tribes would break through and this would herald the end of history.

Whether or not any of this is plausible, the lines certainly refer to the act of defloration. The final couplet, as Christopher Hill first suggested (*Puritanism and Revolution*, 1958, 347, n. 1), recommends that the lovers should not imitate Joshua's sun, which stood still, but David's, which came forth like a bridegroom to run his race. Cf. 'The First Anniversary', ll. 7-8:

> Cromwell alone with greater vigour runs,
> (Sun-like) the stages of succeeding suns . . .

Cromwell resembles the lover in other ways: he could 'ruin the great work of time' ('Horatian Ode', l. 34) and it is also he who 'the force of scattered time contracts, | And in one year the work of ages acts' ('First Anniversary', ll. 13-14).

l. 44. *Thorough*: through.   *gates*: 1681; 'grates' Bodleian MS; 'grates' is preferred by some modern editors, but as Wilcher points out, 'gates of life' is an unexpected, and Marvellian, variant of 'gates of death'.

The unfortunate Lover. The imagery, which is an elaborate distortion of familiar Petrarchan conceits (sighs=gales, tears=seas, etc.), bears some resemblance to a series of emblems depicting a lover's suffering in Otto van Veen, *Amorum Emblemata* (1608). R. L. Colie comments on the emblematic elements in *'My Ecchoing Song'*, 109-13. Cf. also Lovelace's 'Against the Love of Great Ones'.

ll. 6-8. *meteors . . . time*: meteors were thought to be exhalations of vapours from the interior of the earth; they ascended to the sphere of fire and burned out. If they could pass the sphere of fire and the moon they would reach a region of incorruptibility and timelessness.

l. 9. *shipwreck*: the lover's birth, by Caesarian section, is represented as a shipwreck.

l. 16. *section*: three syllables.

ll. 17-19. *tears . . . winds*. The attributes of the Petrarchan lover are explained here by the circumstances of his birth.

l. 22. *forked*: two syllables.

24 l. 26. *masque*: show, representation.

l. 36. *bill*: peck.

l. 38. *consumed*: three syllables.

l. 39. *languished*: three syllables.

l. 40. *amphibium*: a being that lives equally well in water and on land. (The stress is on the third syllable.)

l. 44. *At sharp*: with unbated weapons.

l. 48. *Ajax*: son of Oileus, shipwrecked, stranded, and destroyed by the gods (*Aeneid*, i. 41–5).

ll. 55–6. *And all . . . relish best*. 'Someone commentators take the last line and a half to be the words spoken by the Lover. Donno glosses "says" as a shortened form of "assays". Less violence is done to the text by taking "all he says" as the object of "relish"; the couplet can then be paraphrased: "A lover covered in his own blood can best appreciate everything that this unfortunate lover says"' (Wilcher).

25 l. 57. *banneret*: one created knight on the battlefield. Probably from Lovelace, 'Dialogue—Lucasta, Alexis' in *Lucasta* (1649), to which Marvell contributed commendatory verses (see above, pp. 4–5):

> Love near his standard when his host he sets,
> Creates alone fresh-bleeding bannerets.

After the battle of Edgehill (1642) the word 'must have taken on new life' (Duncan-Jones).

l. 60. *Forced*: disyllabic.

ll. 61–2. *Yet dying . . . ear*. cf. Eccles. 49: 1: 'The remembrance of Josias is like the composition of the perfume that is made by the art of the apothecary . . . and as music at a banquet of wine' (Duncan-Jones).

l. 63. *And he . . . rules*. 'This may mean either "he is supreme in the word of fiction [the romances of chivalry]" or "it is only in the world of fiction that he rules". However, "story" might mean "a painting . . . representing a historical subject. Hence any work of pictorial . . . art containing figures" (*OED*; and cf. "The loyal Scot", l. 171). This would agree better with the next line, and confirm the emblematic character of the poem' (Legouis).

l. 64. *In . . . gules*. Heraldic terms: a red lover in a black field. 'The same contrast of heraldic colours on a blood-stained warrior is found in *Hamlet*, 11. ii. 437–42: Pyrrhus' arms are sable before the massacre; after it he is "total gules"' (Duncan-Jones). Patterson cites a similar figure in Cleveland's *The Character of a London Diurnal* (1647).

The Gallery. Poems describing real or imaginary galleries occur among Marino and his followers, Italian and French, but Marvell uses the trope in a wholly individual way. L. N. Wall (*Notes and Queries*, 202,

170) suggests a debt to Lovelace's 'Amyntor's Grove'. The relation of Marvell's 'paintings' to actual Baroque pictures is considered in Charles H. Hinnant, 'Marvell's Gallery of Art', *Renaissance Quarterly*, 24 (1971).

ll. 7–8. *for . . . mind*: you will find that the mental gallery contains only my pictures of you (all other 'furniture' having been put away).

l. 11. *Examining*: testing.

l. 12. *shop*: business equipment, tools, instruments; '[work]-shopful' (Legouis).

l. 13. *Engines*: instruments (of torture).

l. 14. *cabinet*: picture gallery.

26 l. 24. *perfecting*: stressed on first syllable.

l. 27. *light obscure*. 'A witty glance at the technical term (*chiaroscuro*) for the disposition of brighter and darker masses in a picture' (Wilcher).

l. 35. *halcyons*: these birds were thought to nest on the surface of the water and were thus regarded as ensuring calm at their nesting season.

l. 38. *ambergris*: see 'Bermudas', l. 28.

l. 40. *smell*: sense of smell.

l. 42. *does*: Grierson; 'dost' *1681*; 'do' Bodleian MS.

l. 48. *Whitehall's . . . were*. Charles I had made a great collection of paintings, partly by purchasing those of Vincenzo Gonzaga, Duke of Mantua. The collection was ordered to be sold after the king's death by an act of Parliament (1650). It is argued that Marvell must have written the poem or altered this and the preceding line after 1650. but 'were' may be subjunctive; and in any case the alteration ('are' to 'were') is an easy one.

The Fair Singer. A common theme of the period, occurring in Góngora, the Marinisti, the French poet Voiture ('Sur une belle voix'), and in Carew, Lovelace, Cowley, Stanley, Waller, and Milton.

l. 9. *curled*: disyllabic.

l. 18. *gained*: disyllabic.

Mourning

l. 1. *You . . . the fate*: i.e. astrologers.

l. 3. *infants*: tears; but some editors think 'babies', in the common sense of the image as reflected in the mistress's eyes.

28 l. 9. *moulding of*: 'Taking their shape from the moist spheres (of her eyes)' (Wilcher).

l. 20. *Danae*: she was visited by Jupiter in a shower of gold.

l. 27. *donatives:* largesses 'at the installing of a new' emperor.

l. 29. *wide:* inaccurately.

29 *Daphnis and Chloe.* This poem seems to be related to some lines from Suckling's play *Aglaura* (III. i.) where Aglaura asks Thersames not to consummate their marriage at a critical moment in his life:

> Gather not roses in a wet and frowning hour,
> They'll lose their sweets then, trust me they will, sir,
> What pleasure can love take to play his game out,
> When death must keep the stakes?

(E. E. Duncan-Jones, reported in Leishman, p. 121.) The title is that of the pastoral romance of Longus. The stanza is that of Shakespeare's 'The Phoenix and Turtle', and of Carew's 'Separation of Lovers'.

l. 12. *comprised:* included as a condition.

l. 13. *does use:* is accustomed.

l. 15. *separate:* withdraw from conjugal cohabitation.

30 l. 27. *But . . . more:* but at this point they were mere legacies.

l. 42. *loved:* disyllabic.

l. 44. *resolved:* trisyllabic.

31 l. 53. *condemned:* trisyllabic.

l. 61. *alone:* by itself.

l. 65. *enrich my fate:* by having had her.

32 l. 78. *gourmand Hebrew:* Num. 11: 33, where Jehovah having provided quails and manna strikes the Israelites 'with a very great plague'—presumably as a punishment for eating greedily. (While still wandering in the desert he is due to die.)

l. 79. *with:* Cooke; 'he' *1681.*

l. 80. *He:* Cooke; 'And' *1681.*

l. 83. *seed:* Ferns have no seed; it was once thought that they had, but that the seed was invisible and could confer invisibility on anyone who contrived to get hold of it. ('We have the recipe of fernseed, we walk invisible', 1 *Henry IV*, II. i. 96.)

33 *The Definition of Love.* The title suggests that 'The Definition of Love' belongs to the genre so named, but it is very unlike the other poems which belong to that genre (the most accessible is probably Ralegh's 'Now what is Love') and seems to resemble another kind of poem, which develops the topic 'in love despair is nobler than hope'. Stampa, a follower of Marino, has a poem called 'Amante che si prega di non avere alcuna speranza': 'a noble heart thinks its excellence diminished if hope intrudes its flattering foot to reduce the ardent flames—base

comfort of common minds, depart! He who asks relief values little his gentle torments.' The *Chanson* in which Desportes writes a somewhat similar argument also represents the nobly hopeless love as splendidly contrary to nature, and is that much closer to Marvell. In Marvell's poem, all the dispositions of fate, including the structure of the world, must be altered before the lovers may be joined. John Carey points out that the Latin *definire* means not only 'define', but also 'restrict' or 'limit' (in Patrides).

l. 10. *extended soul:* his soul resides in his mistress, not in him.

34 l. 24. *planisphere:* astrolabe, in which the poles are 'clapt flat together' in the example of 1594 in *OED*. There is a possibility (D. M. Schmitter 'The Cartography of "The Definition of Love"', *Review of English Studies*, 12 (1961), 49–51, and P. Legouis's partly dissenting comment, 51–4) that the figure is terrestrial rather than celestial. Thus the poles would be terrestrial, the planisphere a crushed globe, with the lines of latitude parallel, and those of longitude meeting at the poles. Ann E. Berthoff (*RES*, 17 (1966), 21–5) argues strongly for the celestial interpretation.

ll. 31–2. *conjunction . . . opposition:* astrological terms, the first borrowed for the spiritual union of the lovers, the second also at a remove (the opposition is not between the stars themselves but between the stars and the lovers).

The Picture of Little T. C. in a Prospect of Flowers. See Joseph H. Summers, 'Marvell's "Nature"', *English Literary History*, 20 (1953), 121–35. Margoliouth suggested that T. C. was Theophila Cornewall, born 1644. A year earlier, the same parents had a child, also christened Theophila, who died two days old. If, as Maren-Sofie Røstvig suggests (*Huntington Library Quarterly*, 18 (1954–5), 13 ff.), Marvell borrows from Benlowes' *Theophila*, and if E. E. Duncan-Jones is right in her subsequent conjecture (*Huntington Library Quarterly*, 20 (1955–6), 183–4) that in this title he takes over the literal sense of Benlowes (see note to l. 10), this poem is presumably later than 1652, the date of publication of Benlowes' book. Leishman, (pp. 165–89), traces the tradition of sub-amorous addresses to the pre-pubescent from the Greek Anthology through Homer to the poetry of Marvell's century, and to Prior and Phillips. Cf. 'Young Love' (above, p. 20).

l. 5. *gives them names:* a task traditionally attributed to Eve in Eden.

l. 10. *darling of the gods:* Theophila means 'dear to the gods'.

35 l. 17. *in time:* in good time.

l. 22. *but:* only.

The Match. [Title]. 'The word *match* . . . afforded multiple meanings in seventeenth-century idiom: antagonist, counterpart, equal, contest, pairing, alliance, and, aptly for the second half of the poem, the wick used to ignite gunpowder . . .' (Donno).

36 l. 19. *magazine*: arsenal.

l. 29. *vicinity*: propinquity.

37 *The Mower against Gardens*. The theme of complaint against gardens as wanton human perversion of nature is ancient. There is a rhetorical exercise reported by Seneca the Elder which complains that great houses include streams and woods—*mentita nemora*, fake or 'enforced' (cf. l. 31) groves—within the buildings; that their owners prefer imitations to the real thing and hate what is natural. The art of gardening (grafting, budding, etc.) could be represented as encouraging a sort of botanical adultery; Pliny said so of a fabulous tree of many fruits. The argument as to whether interference with nature is benign was a set piece, a famous version being the debate between Polixenes and Perdita in *A Winter's Tale*, IV. The opposite view of the matter is taken in Thomas Randolph's 'Upon Love fondly refused for Conscience' Sake', a poem in the same rather unusual 'epode' manner—alternating decasyllabic and octosyllabic lines—which uses horticultural 'inoculation' as an argument in favour of fornication. The horticulture of the poem, especially as relating to ll. 27–30, has been much discussed, e.g. by Bradbrook and Thomas, Nicholas A. Salerno, *Études anglaises*, 21 (1968), R. Wilcher, *Études anglaises*, 23 (1970), and John Carey in Patrides (ed.), *Approaches to Marvell*.

l. 1. *Luxurious*: sinful, lecherous.   *bring . . . use*: to reap interest on his vice, to make if profitable (Kermode); spread his vice to other creatures and make it the universal custom (Margoliouth).

l. 6. *standing pool of air*: the phrase is used in books by Henry Wotton (1624) and James Howell (1642).

l. 7. *luscious*: (1) cloying; (2) voluptuous.

l. 8. *stupefied*: (1) astounded; (2) benumbed.

l. 15. *onion root*: bulb.   *did hold*: was valued.

l. 16. *one . . . sold*: tulip bulbs were sold by weight in Holland during the 1630s; one cost 5,500 florins, or as much as 550 sheep (Margoliouth). See Simon Schama, *The Embarrassment of Riches* (1987), 350 ff.

l. 18. *marvel of Peru*. A tropical American plant, *mirabilis jalapa*, called by the botanist Parkinson *mirabilis peruviana* 'the marvel of Peru'.

l. 21. *dealt between*: Tilley records the expression as proverbial for interference between man and wife. It can also mean 'pandered for'.

l. 22. *Forbidden mixtures*: 'Thou shalt not sow thy vineyard with divers seeds: lest the fruit of thy seed, which thou hast sown, and the fruit of thy vineyard, be defiled' (Deut. 22: 9).

l. 24. *tame*: cultivated.

38 l. 25. *uncertain . . . fruit: pirus invito stipite mala tulit* ('the pear bore apples from its unwilling stock'), Propertius, IV. ii. 18.

l. 30. *to procreate without a sex*: there is a long-running argument about the sense here (see references in headnote). But it seems that the cherries are made eunuchs, deprived of their stones. William Harrison (1581) credits gardeners with the power of 'bereaving . . . some . . . fruits of their kernels', and Evelyn, in Marvell's time, says something similar. Carey quotes a passage from Gervase Markham's *The Country Farm* (1616), which explains that stoneless cherries are the result of a graft uniting a young cherry with a barren cherry. Of course this would not be so; but the evidence for the interpretation 'stoneless', though still contested, is strong.

Damon the Mower. The archetypes of such rustic love-complaints are Theocritus, *Idyll* xi, and Virgil, *Eclogue* ii. The mower was socially the lowest of agricultural workers, and it was unusual to substitute him for the shepherd.

l. 2. *Juliana*: i.e. Gillian.

ll. 3–4. *paint . . . scene*: a theatrical figure.

l. 12. *hamstringed*: lamed (by the heat).

39 ll. 19–28. *It from . . . bend*: this description of hot weather is developed from Virgil, *Eclogue* ii.

l. 21. *mads*: Bodleian MS; 'made' *1681*, Margoliouth.

l. 22. *Phaeton*: the charioteer of the sun, who was unable to control it.

l. 28. *gelid*: frozen.

ll. 35–40. *To . . . brought*. The pastoral tradition of such gifts as inducements of love begins, as Leishman points out, with those of Polyphemus to Galatea in *Idyll* xi of Theocritus, elaborated by Ovid in his Polyphemus-Galatea passage, *Metamorphoses*, xiii. 798 ff., and best known from Marlowe's 'Passionate Shepherd to his Love'. There is a particularly charming gift-catalogue in Richard Barnfield's 'Second Day's Lamentation of the Affectionate Shepherd' (1594).

l. 48. *cowslip-water*: used by women to cleanse the skin.

40 ll. 49–56. *What . . . hay.* The Mower is something of a novelty in pastoral, but the rivalry between rustics of different professions is not.

l. 53. *golden*: unlike the sheep's, but resembling Jason's.

l. 54. *closes*: enclosed fields.

l. 57. *Nor . . . sight*: almost literally translated from Virgil's *Eclogue* ii.

25: *nec sum adeo informis*. Leishman rightly remarks that what is so characteristic of Marvell is to transform this by having the speaker look not into a calm sea (as Virgil's Corydon does) but into the curved and polished blade of his scythe.

l. 64. *ring*: the 'fairy ring', which is actually caused by the mycelium of certain fungi.

41   l. 83. *shepherd's purse: Capsella bursa-pastoris*, a weed supposed to check bleeding.   *clown's-all-heal: Stachys palustris*, said to heal wounds.

The Mower to the Glow-worms.

l. 1. *lamps:* 'You will make me believe that glow-worms are lanterns'. This proverb (Tilley G 143) is cited by Kitty Scoular, *Natural Magic* (1965), 106.

ll. 7–8. *Shining . . . fall:* 'Glowbards never appear before hay is ripe upon the ground, nor yet after it is cut down' (Pliny, *Natural History*, XI. 28, tr. Philemon Holland; quoted by Leishman, 125). Kitty Scoular (107) points to an exact parallel in Remy Belleau, for whom the insect is also the countryman's prophet:

> Qui au laboureur prophétise
> Qu'il faut pour faucher, qu'il aguise
> Sa faulx, et face les moissons.

l. 9. *officious:* attentive.

l. 12. *foolish fires: Ignis Fatuus*, will-o'-the-wisp; marsh-gas (methane) spontaneously ignited.

42   *The Mower's Song*

l. 1. *survey:* a coloured estate map (Craze).

ll. 3–4. *And in . . . glass:* green was traditionally the colour of hope.

43   *Ametas and Thestylis making Hay-ropes.* Probably meant to be sung, like the other pastoral dialogues. Colie (54) has a good comment on this poem.

l. 10. *yourselves:* Bodleian MS.; 'yourself (your selve)' *1681*, Margoliouth.

Music's Empire. For the relation of this poem to the *laus musicae* tradition see James Hutton, 'Some English Poems in Praise of Music', *English Miscellany*, 2 (Rome, 1951), and John Hollander, *The Untuning of the Sky: Ideas of Music in English Poetry, 1500–1700* (Princeton, 1961).

44   l. 5. *Jubal:* 'The father of all such as handle the harp and organ' (Gen. 4: 21).

l. 6. *jubilee:* (Jewish) year of emancipation and restoration; more generally, a season of joyful celebration. Did Marvell associate the ritual Jubilee with Jubal?

l. 7. *sullen:* gloomy.

ll. 9–12. *Each sought . . . withdrew.* These lines may reflect Davenant's *Gondibert* (1651), II. vi. 80, which has 'virgin trebles' and 'manly voice' (Craze).

l. 9. *consort:* (1) mate; (2) harmony.

l. 16. *choir:* this word may be a verb (cf. *Merchant of Venice*, V. i. 62), as Craze argues. (Then, of course, we should read, 'heavens choir'.)

l. 17. *mosaic:* presenting a unity made up of diverse sound.

l. 22. *conqueror:* Margoliouth suggests Fairfax, comparing the following line with 'Upon the Hill and Grove', ll. 75–6. Hollander argues for Cromwell.

The Garden. Like 'The Mower against Gardens', this poem is always confronting a silent set of antithetical attitudes, and from this derives its wit. Like Adam, the poet is placed *in paradiso deliciarum*, in a paradise of delights, and like him he has a duty to contemplate them. The resemblance to Adam, we are told, is rather to the man alone, to the period before Eve's creation; the poet echoes St Ambrose's misogyny and Joseph Hall's 'I do not find that man, thus framed, found the want of a helper. His fruition of God gave him fulness of contentment.' The points are made within the large context of garden topics. The poet makes the green of the garden stand for solitude against crowds, retirement against action, sensual delight free of sexual pursuit, the satisfaction of the sense against that of the mind. Perhaps Marvell was thinking of Randolph—the opening stanza of that poet's 'Pastoral Courtship', at any rate, introduces an antithetical garden, in which all trees combine to form, not the garland of repose, but a bower for lovemaking:

> Behold these woods, and mark, my sweet,
> How all the boughs together meet.
> The cedar his fair arms displays,
> And mixes branches with the bays.
> The lofty pine deigns to descend,
> And sturdy oaks do gentle bend,
> One with another subtly weaves
> Into one loom the various leaves,
> As all ambitious were to be
> Mine and my Phyllis' canopy!

Marvell's second stanza plays wittily on the plants as virtues, a theme familiar in biblical commentary, and on the old paradox that solitude can be more pleasantly companionable than company. By the same token, it is more amorous than love, a paradox stated in terms

of the emblematic colours of solitude and love. Ever since Ovid's
Oenone pastoral, lovers have cut the name of the desired person on
trees; what we should do, it seems to follow, is to cut on trees their
own names. Gods chase girls not for sex but to turn them into trees.
And so the paradoxes continue. The figures of natural abundance are
as old as Hesiod; like Adam, the solitary has easily what others must
labour for; and unlike Adam, he may fall without being greatly upset.
However, neither for him nor Adam is sensual repletion all; the
garden provides no more than a mirror of creation, since it also
enables the mind to withdraw from sensibilia and produce its own
fantasies, establishing worlds other than the visible. Thus begins a
formal garden ecstasy; but there is still an element of antithesis carried
over from the earlier wit: this ascending love is traditionally, in the
familiar Platonic formula, contrasted with that which descends to
mere sensual contact. The soul, ascended, is as it were between the
worlds, like a bird on a bough. It is poised between the white light of
eternity, and the varieties of colour that light assumes in the creation.
This, we learn, was the position of Adam before Eve and the Fall;
there is a newly witty reprise of the earlier antitheses on love. After
this exercise comes a quiet close, but it is still constructed as an
antithesis. Other sundials boast that they count only sunny hours,
depending on the unmediated light of direct sunshine; this one, which
is a new kind of sundial (he is calling the garden a sundial), reckons
hours much more sweet and wholesome; its light is filtered through
the greenness of trees and so is 'milder'. Its face consists not of figures
cut in stone, but flowers, which yield to us, as to the bee, sweetness
and light.

The Latin version, 'Hortus', is not throughout a translation, nor yet
an original, but partly an exercise in a related mode (see G.
Williamson, 'Marvell's "Hortus" and "Garden"' in *Milton and Others*,
1965).

l. 1. *vainly:* (1) futilely; (2) arrogantly (Donno).

l. 2. *the palm . . . bays:* rewards for achievement in war, statesmanship,
poetry.

45 l. 6. *upbraid:* (1) censure; (2) braid up (Donno).

l. 7. *all . . . all:* as opposed to the 'single' of l. 4; retirement offers
greater rewards.   *close:* unite.

l. 14. *plants:* i.e. the plants symbolizing them, as palm, oak, and bays
symbolize the various activities of l. 2.

ll. 15-16. *Society . . . solitude:* a paradox: ordinarily it is society that is
thought of as 'polished'. The paradox goes back to Scipio's *nunquam
minus solus quam cum solus.*

l. 17. *white . . . red:* emblematic of female and beauty.

l. 18. *amorous:* beautiful, worthy of love. *green:* by association, emblematic of rural and solitary retirement.

ll. 19–20. *Fond lovers . . . name.* Ralph Austen, *Observations on Sir Francis Bacon's Natural History,* 1658, says one can inscribe young trees so that later 'the letters or figures will be more plain' (Colie, 159).

l. 24. *No . . . own:* if lovers behave thus to celebrate woman's beauty, it is logical—since the trees are more beautiful than the women—to carve only the tree's name on the tree.   *your:* Cooke; 'you' *1681.*

l. 25. *heat:* (1) ardour; (2) race.

l. 26. *retreat:* (1) a military and (2) a religious figure.

l. 28. *Still:* always.

ll. 29–32. *Apollo . . . reed.* In the myth, Apollo is thwarted when Daphne turns into a laurel, and Pan when Syrinx turns into a reed; Marvell inverts the myths to establish the 'amorous' superiority of trees to women.

ll. 33–40. *What . . . grass:* in this paradise, as in that of Adam, one is exposed to all sensual delight, but here one can be ensnared and fall without serious consequences. The catalogue of readily available fruit is a commonplace with a long history.

46 l. 41. *Meanwhile . . . less:* experiencing less pleasure in nature than the delighted senses do (and so turning upwards). According to Aristotle, *de Anima,* i. iv, 'the mind is less subject to passion'.   *pleasure: 1681;* 'pleasures' Bodleian MS.

l. 43. *that ocean:* alluding to the belief that there is in the sea a parallel creation for everything on land. The implied theory of knowledge is that we can know the world because of the pre-existence of related forms in our minds.

l. 44. *straight:* at once.

ll. 45–6. *Yet . . . seas:* but the mind does more than merely provide such correspondences; the fancy or imagination can create forms which have no equivalent in reality.

ll. 47–8. *Annihilating . . . shade:* making the created world seem as nothing compared with what can be imagined by the retired contemplative.

l. 49. *Here . . . foot:* cf. 'Upon Appleton House', l. 645.

l. 54. *whets:* preens.

l. 55. *And . . . flight:* resting, as it were, between the created and the intelligible worlds in the process of its Platonic ascent; the same figure in a similar context is used by Spenser, 'Hymn of Heavenly Beauty', ll. 22–8.

l. 56. *various light:* the neo-Platonic image (familiar to all from Shelley's 'Adonais') was common enough in the Renaissance: see, e.g., Chapman, 'Ovid's Banquet of Sense', stanza 55.

ll. 57-8. *Such . . . mate:* the Garden of Eden was like this before the introduction of Eve; a point earlier made by St Ambrose (*Epistles*, i. 49).

l. 60. *What other . . . meet:* 'And the Lord God said, It is not good that the man should be alone; I will make a help meet for him' (Gen. 2: 18). The words were later conflated giving 'helpmate'.

l. 66. *dial:* sundial. We suspect that here the whole garden is meant; it is metaphorically a sundial; hence 'new'—a new version of the sundial.

ll. 67-8. *Where from . . . zodiac run:* the sun is made milder because in this 'floral zodiac' the sunlight is filtered through the trees, on to plants.

47 l. 70. *time:* a pun. The clock enables us to tell the time and enables the bee to take nectar from thyme. Marvell gets this point into his Latin version also.

The second Chorus from Seneca's Tragedy 'Thyestes'. Compare Cowley's translation of the same passage from *Several Discourses by Way of Essays, in Verse and Prose*, iii, 'Of Obscurity' (1668):

> Upon the slippery tops of human state,
>   The guilded pinnacles of fate,
> Let others proudly stand, and for a while
>   The giddy danger to beguile,
> With joy, and with disdain look down on all,
>   Till their heads turn, and down they fall.
> Me, O ye gods, on earth, or else so near
>   That I no fall to earth may fear,
> And, O ye gods, at a good distance seat
>   From the long ruins of the great.
> Here wrapped in the arms of quiet let me lie;
> Quiet, companion of obscurity.
> Here let my life, with as much silence slide
>   As time that measures it does glide.
> Nor let my homely death embroidered be
>   With scutcheon or with elegy.
>   An old plebeian let me die,
> Alas, all then are such as well as I.
>   To him, alas, to him, I fear,
> The face of death will terrible appear:
> Who in his life flattered his senseless pride

> By being known to all the world beside,
> Does not himself, when he is dying, know,
> Nor what he is nor whither he's to go.

Sir Matthew Hale also has a version, in *Contemplations, Moral and Divine* (1676).

Title: Donno; 'Senec. Traged. ex Thyeste Chor. 2.' *1681*.

l. 2. *Tottering favour's pinnacle: 1681*; 'Giddy favour's slippery hill' Bodleian MS.

An Epitaph upon Frances Jones. Frances Jones's epitaph in the crypt of St Martin-in-the-Fields shows that Frances Jones was the daughter of Arthur Jones and Katherine Boyle, Lady Ranelagh, daughter of the Earl of Cork. Frances was born in 1633, and died in 1672. (See Hugh Brogan, 'Marvell's *Epitaph on—*', *Renaissance Quarterly*, 32, (1979), 197–8.) Lady Ranelagh was a frequent visitor to Milton when he was living in Petty France, as, too, was Marvell.

Title: this edn.; 'An Epitaph on—' *1681*.

48 l. 14. *came and went:* i.e. in prayer.

Upon the Hill and Grove at Bilbrough. For similar poems on mountains, see Kitty Scoular, *Natural Magic*, pp. 154 ff. In part an exercise in a manner much more fully developed in 'Upon Appleton House'. Bilbrough was a house of Fairfax's near Nun Appleton. Thomas Fairfax (1612–71), the third baron, had been commander-in-chief of the Parliamentary army. He refused to condone the execution of the king, and resigned in June 1650 because he disapproved of the proposed campaign against the Scots, which Cromwell undertook. Fairfax then retired to his Yorkshire properties, where he led the life of the great landowner who was also a scholar and a poet. He had married Ann Vere, who came of a distinguished military family, in 1637; she appears to have been an imposing woman of strong Presbyterian faith. In 1651 they appointed Marvell tutor to their daughter Mary, and he seems to have remained with them at Nun Appleton and Bilbrough for two years. Related to this poem is the Latin 'Epigramma in duos montes' printed before it in *1681*.

l. 5. *pencil:* paintbrush.   *draw:* paint.

l. 7. *model:* i.e. in its perfect circularity.

l. 13. *For:* on account of.

l. 14. *new centre:* Because the irregularity of the mountains has made the earth imperfectly spherical.

49 l. 28. *Tenerifc:* Volcanic peak in Canary Islands (12,192 ft). Bilbrough is 145 ft.

l. 29. *seamen:* they used the hill as a landmark for entering the Humber.

l. 34. *plume:* Cooke; it means 'crest' here; 'plum' *1681.* 'plum' Margoliouth.

l. 36. *sacred:* clumps of trees so placed were often thought of as sacred groves.

l. 38. *Of the great . . . terror:* the authority of Fairfax.

l. 43. *Vera:* Ann Vere, Lady Fairfax.

50 l. 56. *this:* i.e. this lord.

l. 73. *ye:* Bodleian MS; 'the' *1681.*

l. 74. *oak:* referring to the sacred oak at Dodona, from the rustlings of whose leaves the will of Zeus could be discovered.

51 *Upon Appleton House.* Marvell seems to have spent some two years (1650–2) as tutor to Maria Fairfax at Nun Appleton, the seat of Thomas, Lord Fairfax. The received idea of the house was until 1972 based on the account of it in C. R. Markham's *Life of the Great Lord Fairfax* (1870), 365, but it now seems likely that the building he describes was put up later, and that in Marvell's time the family lived in what remained of the nunnery. The new house was large, modern, and grand; its predecessor much humbler, which makes the opening stanzas of the poem more appropriate. (See John Newman, letter in *TLS,* 28 Jan. 1972, and further comment by A. A. Tait, *TLS,* 11 Feb. 1972.) The original house belonged to a Cistercian priory, and was acquired by the Fairfax family at the dissolution in 1542. Some nunnery ruins remain. Marvell's poem is a somewhat anomalous member of the genre of poems about country houses.

The poem, which certainly has allusions to the recent civil wars, has lately been treated as a political or political-apocalyptic allegory, with much questioning as to whether Marvell was criticizing Fairfax's retirement. See e.g. Margarita Stocker's exaggeratedly eschatological *Apocalyptic Marvell* (1986), 46–66, and Ernest B. Gilman, *The Curious Perspective* (1978), 204–31, an interesting account of Marvell's non-committed style, which denies the reader a fixed point of view. The best study of the political setting is Michael Wilding, *Dragons Teeth* (1987), 138–72.

To my Lord Fairfax. For Fairfax, see note on 'Upon the Hill and Grove', above (p. 141).

ll. 1–8. *Within . . . gazed:* this somewhat chauvinistic praise for the modesty of Nun Appleton is probably intended to be a criticism of poems praising the architectural grandeur of a patron's house; specifically, perhaps, Saint-Amant's praise of the Duc de Retz's hunting lodge in his *Palais de la Volupté:*

> L'invention en est nouvelle,
> Et ne vient que d'une cervelle

> *Qui fait tout avec tant de poids,*
> *Et prend de tout si bien le chois*
> *Qu'elle met en claire évidence*
> *Que sa grandeur et sa prudence*
> *Sont aussi dignes, sans mentir,*
> *De régner comme de batir.*

ll. 5–6. *Who . . . gazed:* who, in agony to bring his great design to birth, employed his skull as a model for the vault.

l. 8. *arch:* architectural pun.

l. 12. *equal:* appropriate (to their size).

l. 22. *mote:* Bodleian MS; 'mose' *1681*; 'mole' Cooke.

l. 24. *the first builders:* of the tower of Babel (Gen. 11: 1–9).

52 l. 30. *loop:* opening.

l. 31. *door so strait:* Matt. 7: 13.

l. 36. *Vere:* Anne Vere, Fairfax's wife.

l. 40. *As Romulus's . . . cell:* the thatched hut in which Romulus, founder of Rome, had lived, here is compared to a beehive.

l. 45. *immure:* enclose.

l. 46. *The circle . . . quadrature:* a reference to the old problem of squaring the circle. See R. L. Colie, 'Some Paradoxes in the Language of Things' in J. A. Mazzeo (ed.), *Reason and the Imagination* (1962), 121–3. The problem became the standard trope for time-wasting intellectual activity'. But to live by the square of human constancy, and respect the circle of heaven (the circle a symbol of God), is 'holy mathematics'.

l. 56. *That:* its humility.

53 l. 64. *invent:* find out.

l. 65. *frontispiece of poor:* the door is conceived as the frontispiece of a book, and the poor, confidently expecting the alms of Fairfax, are its decoration.

l. 71. *inn:* a reference to some lines of Fairfax, preserved in the Bodleian Library, called 'Upon the newbuilt house at Appleton':

> Think not, O man that dwells herein
> This house's a stay but as an inn
> Which for convenience fittly stands
> In way to one not made with hands
> But if time here thou take rest
> Yet think eternity's the best.

l. 73. *Bishop's Hill:* Fairfax's house in York.   *Denton:* another Fairfax estate thirty miles from Nun Appleton.

l. 90. *Thwaites:* Isabella Thwaites married an ancestor of Fairfax. She had been left in the charge of the Prioress of Nun Appleton, who tried, by shutting her up, to prevent her marriage to Sir William Fairfax; but her authority was overriden, and the marriage took place in 1518.

54 l. 105. *white:* the colour of the Cistercian habit.

ll. 107-8. *And our . . . dim:* a reference to the parable of the wise and foolish virgins (Matt. 25: 1-13).

l. 121. *prayed:* two syllables.

l. 122. *legend:* a saint's life.

55 l. 141. *crown:* of lilies.

l. 152. devoto: religious devotee.

56 l. 169. *nice:* fastidious.

l. 172. *perfecting:* stressed on the first syllable.

l. 180. *sea-born amber:* ambergris (see 'Bermudas', l. 28), used to perfume linen in storage.

l. 181. *grieved:* hurt, wounded.   *pastes:* pastries.

l. 182. *baits:* refreshments.

l. 184. *These . . . confess:* i.e. unless they needed a priest as confessor.

57 ll. 197-9. *Now . . . begin:* i.e. Now claim her plighted word, from which religion (which she henceforward doth begin) has released her' (Margoliouth).

l. 216. *And vice . . . wall:* so that the stone, even though laid by a just hand, would not fall on the girl's seducer, simply because it has been infected by the vice of the inmates of the nunnery.

58 l. 221. *state:* estate.

l. 232. *First from a judge . . . soldier:* Sir William Fairfax's father was a judge; his mother the daughter of Lord Roos, a distinguished soldier.

l. 233. *in the storm:* in taking her from the nunnery by force.

ll. 241-4. *Is . . . Germany:* Sir Thomas, son of this pair, fought in Germany, and his son in France; a son of the next generation fought in Germany and was Marvell's patron in France.

l. 244. *either Germany:* i.e. high (Germany) and the low countries.

l. 245. *one:* probably an allusion to the present Lord Fairfax, a general of the victorious Parliamentary army.

l. 248. *would intercept:* wished to interrupt (the family succession).

59 l. 253. *disjointed:* distracted.

l. 268. *had:* Bodleian MS; 'hath' *1681*, Margoliouth.

l. 274. *escheat:* a legal term: if the tenant died without an heir, the estate reverted to the lord.

ll. 281–2. *From that blest bed . . . fame:* it is uncertain whether 'hero' means Sir Thomas Fairfax, son of this marriage, or Lord Fairfax, Marvell's employer.

60 l. 288. *every sense:* there were gardens so laid out in sixteenth-century France.

l. 292. dian: reveille.

l. 295. *pan:* the part of the musket lock holding the priming.

l. 296. *flask:* powder-flask (the flowers represented as infantrymen).

l. 301. *virgin nymph:* Mary Fairfax.

l. 303. *think:* imperative (addressed to the flowers).   *not compare:* do not invite comparison with.

l. 305. *firemen:* soldiers using firearms (as distinct, for example, from bowmen).

61 l. 320. *or: 1681;* 'nor' Cooke; 'or' must mean 'ere': 'before asking the password'.

l. 322. *garden of the world:* for this familiar topic (England as garden of the world) see J. W. Bennett, 'Britain among the Fortunate Isles', *Studies in Philology* 53 (1956), 114 ff., and Leishman, 283 ff.

l. 323. *four:* disyllabic.

l. 326. *flaming sword:* Gen. 3: 24.

l. 328. *thee:* Bodleian MS; 'The' *1681*, Margoliouth.

l. 330. *militia:* four syllables.

l. 336. *Switzers:* referring to the yellow and red stripes of the papal Swiss guards.

l. 341. *stoves:* hot houses.

l. 345. *there:* Bodleian MS; 'their' *1681*, Margoliouth.

62 l. 349. *Cinque Ports:* a group of ancient ports on the south-east coast of England. The wardenship was an important military appointment. Fairfax served as warden 1650–1.

l. 351. *half-dry:* because of the gradual extension of the land, which progressively cut off some of these ports from the sea. Fairfax was not nominally warden, but exercised the power of the warden by virtue of his being a member of the Council.

l. 356. *earthy:* Bodleian MS; 'earthly' *1681*, Margoliouth.   *want:* lack.

l. 358. *As that . . . shrinks:* the sensitive plant.

l. 363. *Cawood Castle:* until 1642, a seat of the Archbishop of York, about two miles from Nun Appleton.

l. 365. *quarrelled:* found fault with.

l. 368. *gaze: 1681,* Margoliouth; 'graze' Bodleian MS.

l. 372. *giants:* 'And there we saw the giants . . . and we were in our own sight as grasshoppers, and so we were in their sight' (Num. 13: 33).

l. 380. *Whether . . . go:* whether he is falling or walking.

63   l. 382. *the ground:* mud or sand from the seabed.

l. 385. *No scene . . . strange:* referring to the elaborate machinery of the Renaissance theatre. For details see L. B. Campbell, *Scenes and Machines on the English Stage* (Cambridge, 1923), and Richard Southern, *Changeable Scenery* (1952).

ll. 389–90. *Who seem . . . green sea:* E. E. Duncan-Jones cites Wisd. 19: 7: 'where water stood before, dry land appeared; and out of the Red sea a way without impediment: and out of the violent stream a green field'.

l. 392. *And crowd . . . side:* crowd to either side to form a lane.

l. 395. *rail:* corncrake or landrail. Cf. Virgil, *Georgics, iv.* 510–12, where a ploughman kills a baby nightingale.

l. 399. *untimely mowed:* cf. 'Damon the Mower', l. 88.

l. 401. *Thestylis:* the name comes from virgil, *Eclogues,* ii. 10–11; there she cooks for the reapers.

l. 402. *mowing camp:* as the mowers are represented as soldiers, Thestylis is a camp follower.   *cates:* food.

l. 406. *He:* the poet. This extremely unusual effect—a character in the poem jokes with the poet as if she had read the preceding verses and can develop the scriptural allusion—is well described by Frank J. Warnke as 'cracking the frame of fiction' (in Patrides, ed.).

l. 408. *Rails rain . . . dew:* Exod. 16: 13–14.

64   l. 416. *sourdine:* mute on trumpet producing hoarse effect.

l. 417. *Or:* either.

l. 419. *traverse:* a stage curtain on which a scene was depicted, but here used metaphorically for a track across a field.

l. 426. *hay:* (1) country dance; (2) mown grass.

l. 428. *Alexander's sweat:* had a 'passing delightful savour' (Plutarch, *Life of Alexander*).

l. 430. *fairy circles:* the effect of mycelium. See 'Damon the Mower', l. 64.

l. 437. *Memphis:* Egyptian city near the Pyramids.

l. 439. *Roman camps:* tumuli, now known to be of British origin.

l. 441. *This scene ... withdrawing brings:* continuing the theatrical figure of l. 385.

l. 442. *face:* aspect.

l. 444. *cloths:* canvases.   *Lely:* Sir Peter Lely, celebrated Dutch portrait painter, who came to England in 1641.

65 l. 446. *table rase: tabula rasa* (blank tablet).

l. 447. *toril*: A reminiscence of Marvell's visit to Spain, but by 'toril' he means 'bull-ring' and not the bull's enclosure, which is the modern sense.

l. 448. *Madril:* Madrid.

l. 450. *Levellers:* egalitarian political movement of the period, favouring levelling out differences in rank, parliamentary representation, etc. Fairfax had suppressed a Leveller movement at Burford in 1649. *take pattern at:* use as a model.

l. 451. *in common:* not only is the meadow level, it is also a common for grazing, which strengthens its use as a model to levellers.

l. 453. *increased:* grew.

l. 454. *beast*: Bodleian MS; 'breast' *1681*.

l. 456. *Davenant ... herd:* Sir William Davenant, a contemporary of Marvell's, describes in his admired experimental epic, the unfinished *Gondibert*, a painting of the six days of creation. On the sixth day a 'universal herd' appears (II. vi. 60). The reference carries on the comparison with the new-created world begun in ll. 445–6.

l. 458. *A landskip ... looking-glass:* a landscape shown in a painting as reflected in a looking glass and thus reduced in size.

ll. 461–2. *Such fleas ... lie:* so do fleas appear on the glass before one looks at them through the microscope. Leishman cites James Howell's *Epistolae Ho-Elianae:* 'such glasses as anatomists use in the dissection of bodies, which can make a flea look like a cow'; and John Carey says Marvell is making fun of Howell: 'If fleas, when magnified, really look like cows ... then it follows that unmagnified fleas can't look like fleas at all but like very, very tiny cows ... what Howell had at the end of his "Multiplying Glasses" was a midget dairy herd, and that is why Marvell, seeing a midget dairy herd, likens it not just to fleas, but to fleas waiting in Howell's multiplying glasses to be magnified and identified by him as cows' (in Patrides, ed.).

l. 466. *Denton:* see note to l. 73.

l. 472. *And isles ... round:* makes an island around.

l. 476. *leeches:* refers to the superstition that horsehair in water turned into eels or leeches.

66 ll. 477–80. *How boats . . . pound:* cf. Ovid, *Metamorphoses,* i. 295–6.

l. 485. *the first carpenter:* Noah.

l. 486. *pressed:* commandeered.

l. 490. *union:* the two woods are joined at one point, just as the Vere and Fairfax pedigrees are joined.

l. 491. *pedigrees:* genealogical trees.

l. 493. *in war:* they were cut down to meet a wartime demand for timber.

ll. 495–6. *And . . . expect:* cf. Saint-Amant, 'La Solitude', ll. 6–10:

> . . . ces bois, qui se trouverent
> A la nativite du temps,
> Et que tous les siecles reverent,
> Estre encore aussi beaux et vers,
> Qu'aux premiers jours de l'univers.

l. 499. *neighbourhood:* proximity.

l. 502. *fifth:* of a different substance from the existing four (earth, air, fire, and water).

ll. 505–12. *Dark . . . fires:* this is part of Marvell's considerable debt to Benlowes. See M.S. Røstvig, *The Happy Man* (Oslo, 1954), 247–8.

l. 508. *Corinthian:* the most ornate of the Greek architectural orders.

67 l. 526. *Sad pair . . . moan:* imitated from Virgil's *nec gemere aeria cessabit turtur ab ulmo* ('and the turtle-dove shall not cease moaning from the high elm'), *Eclogues,* i. 58.

l. 535. *stork-like:* the stork was held to leave behind one of its young as a tribute to the owner; the heron is imagined as dropping one young bird in similar tribute.

l. 537. *hewel's:* green woodpecker's.

l. 538. *holt-felster's:* woodcutter's.

68 l. 568. *inverted tree:* 'Man is like an inverted tree' is a commonplace explored by A. B. Chambers (*Studies in the Renaissance,* 8 (1961), 291–9), where it is traced back to Aristotle and even to Plato (*Timaeus,* 90A—the same work, 91E, may be the original of ll. 565–6). A famous example is Swift, *Meditation on a Broomstick.*

69 l. 577. *Sybil's leaves:* palm leaves from which the Romans foretold the future.

l. 580. *Like Mexique . . . plumes:* pictures made by sticking feathers together.

l. 582. *mosaic:* an image assembled from various (natural) materials; but also with a reference to the 'Mosaic' books. Of the two books of God—the Bible and Nature—Nature is the 'lighter'.

l. 586. *mask:* an allegorical garb, as for some masque-like entertainment.

l. 591. *antic cope:* cf. Milton's *Apology for Smectymnuus (Complete Prose Works*, New Haven, 1953, i. 930); 'cope' means 'ecclesiastical outer garment'.

l. 592. *prelate:* also developed from the Latin of Benlowes.

l. 599. *shed:* separate, part.

70 l. 610. *gadding vines:* a reminiscence of Milton's 'Lycidas', l. 40.

ll. 629–30. *No . . . Nile:* referring to the belief that the Nile floods begot serpents and crocodiles from the mud (cf. *Antony and Cleopatra*, II. vii. 29–31).

l. 631. *itself:* the river.

l. 636. *slick:* sleek.

71 l. 639. *shade:* reflected image.

l. 640. *Narcissus-like:* Narcissus was in love with his own reflection in a pool.

l. 649. *quills:* floats.

l. 650. *angles:* fishing tackle.   *utensils:* accent on first syllable.

l. 651. *Maria:* Mary Fairfax, to whom Marvell was tutor.

l. 659. *whisht:* hushed.

l. 660. *bonne mine:* Good appearance; puts on its best behaviour (*bonne* is disyllabic).

l. 668. *eben shuts:* ebony (black) shutters.

72 l. 669. *halcyon:* this bird produces absolute calm. See 'The Gallery', l. 35, though here the bird is the kingfisher. Virgil (*Georgics*, iii. 335 ff.) describes its appearance in the calm of evening. Hodges remarks that Pliny (*History of the World*, tr. Philemon Holland, 1634, I. x. 32) offers two alternatives: the halcyon either *makes* the calm, or it knows when the calm will occur. Marvell chooses the first, slightly more magical explanation.

l. 671. *horror:* awe, reverence (Latinism).

l. 673. *she:* the halcyon.

l. 677. *stupid:* stupefied.

l. 679. *assist:* attend; are present at.

l. 680. *sapphire-winged mist:* the kingfisher in flight.

ll. 681–2. *Maria . . . evening hush:* the influence of a lady over a landscape, especially an evening landscape, is a poetic theme discussed by Leishman, 81 ff., and Scoular, 147 (with parallel from Théophile de Viau) and 172 ff.

l. 684. *star new-slain*: a meteor, thought to be 'exhaled' from the earth (l. 686).

l. 688. *vitrified*: turned to glass, as in the incorruptible crystalline sphere of the fixed stars; or, like the 'sea of glass' described in Rev. 4: 6.

73 l. 708. *all the languages*: Mary Fairfax, under Marvell's tuition, was proving a capable linguist.

l. 714. *trains*: (1) plots, stratagems; (2) trains of artillery.

l. 724. *the starry Vere*: perhaps a reference to the Vere coat of arms.

74 l. 733. *grin*: grimace.

l. 734. *black-bag*: mask.

l. 738. *line*: lineage.

l. 744. *choice*: Mary Fairfax later married the profligate Duke of Buckingham.

l. 753. *Thessalian Tempe*: the vale of Tempe in Thessaly was a famous ancient 'paradise'.

l. 755. *Aranjuez*: Spanish royal gardens on the Tagus, south of Madrid.

l. 756. *Bel-Retiro*: Buen Retiro, another royal residence near Madrid.

l. 757. *Idalian Grove*: Cyprus, the garden of Venus.

l. 761. *'Tis . . . world*: referring to the disorder of a fallen world, to be compared with the order and balance of the microcosm, or little world, of Nun Appleton, which reflects the state of the world before paradise was lost.

75 l. 771. *Antipodes in shoes*: those who dwell directly opposite us on the globe (their feet pointing to our feet).

l. 772. *Have shod . . . canoes*: coracles ('leather boats') were so carried. There was a Cambridge student song about lawyers, which had a similar point (Craze, 252).

l. 774. *rational amphibii*: amphibii are animals at home in and out of water; the salmon-fishers, men being 'rational animals', are rational amphibii. Cf. Sir Thomas Browne, *Religio Medici*, i. 34: 'man that great and true amphibium'.

l. 776. *Does now . . . appear*: in being covered by a hemisphere of darkness, like the boat on the salmon-fisher's head.

Flecknoe, an English Priest at Rome. Richard Flecknoe, Roman Catholic priest and minor poet, was in Rome during 1645 and 1646, when Marvell may have met him. Flecknoe was later satirized as the reigning prince of Dulness in Dryden's *Mac Flecknoe*. Marvell's encounter with him is somewhat in the manner of Donne's *Satires*. The poem may have been written soon after the meeting but remained unpublished until *1681*.

l. 3. *Melchizedek*: King of Salem and priest of the most high God (Gen. 14: 18); also a prophetic type of Christ.

l. 4. *Lord Brooke*: Fulke Greville, first Lord Brook (1554–1628). Flecknoe published verses complimenting Brooke's *Works* (published in 1670).

l. 6. *The Sad Pelican*: the Pelican was a common inn sign.   *subject divine*: the pelican was thought to feed its young with its own flesh and blood; it became a symbol for Christ. See ll. 127–8.

l. 8. *triple property*: another reference to the joke about Melchizedek.

l. 12. *ceiling*: (1) wall-hanging; (2) wainscot.   *sheet*: (1) bedsheet; (2) winding sheet.

l. 14. *show*: appear.

l. 18. *stanzas*: rooms (It.).   *appartement*: suite of rooms (Fr.) (four syllables).

l. 19. *information*: five syllables.

l. 20. *and*: *1681*, Margoliouth; 'in' Bodleian MS.

76 l. 26. *prepared*: three syllables.

l. 28. *The last . . . brain*: a reminiscence of Milton's 'Lycidas', l. 70–1:

> Fame is the spur that the clear spirit doth raise
> (That last infirmity of noble mind)

l. 43. *straitness*: tension.

l. 53. *he was sick*: and thereby exempt from the Ordinance.

l. 54. *the ordinance*: against eating meat in Lent.

l. 55. *him scant*: G. A. Aitken, *Satires*; 'him: Scant' *1681*.   *scant*: fasting.

l. 57. *our dinner*: Bodleian MS; 'dinner' *1681*.

l. 63. *basso relievo*: low relief (It.).

77 ll. 64–5. *Who as a camel . . . stitch*: Matt. 19–24.   *stitch*: (1) grimace of pain; (2) shred of clothing; (3) in sewing (Donno).

l. 66. *rich*: to be rich is what makes it as difficult to enter heaven as for a camel to go through the eye of a needle (Mark 10: 25; Luke 18: 25).

l. 69. *circumscribes*: wraps himself in writing.

l. 74. *sottana:* cassock (It.).

l. 75. *antic:* (1) old (antique); (2) grotesque; (3) crazy.

l. 76. *first Council of Antioch:* AD 264.

l. 78. *tradition:* the authority of unwritten tradition, held by Roman Catholics to be equal to that of the Scriptures, was an important difference between Catholic and Protestant; it underlies this joke.

l. 83. *disfurnish:* i.e. of its occupants (the only furniture).

l. 90. *thorough:* through.

l. 92. *the palace:* E. E. Duncan-Jones suggests the Casa Barberini, the Cardinal of that name being Protector of the English in Rome.

l. 98. *Delightful:* delighted.

l. 99. *penetration:* the occupation of the same space by two bodies at the same time (cf. 'Horatian Ode', l. 42).

l. 100. *Two . . . three:* 'When two or three are gathered together in thy name . . .' (Book of Common Prayer).

l. 101. *in one substance:* like the Trinity.

78 l. 126. *Nero's poem:* Suetonius tells us that 'no one was allowed to leave the theatre during his recital', however pressing the need (*Nero*, 23).

l. 130. *foul copies:* rough drafts (and the more obvious sense).

l. 136 *ordinaries:* inns.

l. 137. *chancres and poulains:* syphilitic sores.

79 l. 152. *Perillus:* the contriver of the Brazen Bull of Phalaris, and its first victim.

l. 156. *is no lie:* does not give you the lie (require you to challenge him).

l. 170. *for a vow:* as an *ex voto* offering

An Horatian Ode upon Cromwell's Return from Ireland. This poem was cancelled from all extant copies of *1681* except for two, one in the British Library and one in the Huntington Library, California.

Cromwell returned from his ferocious reconquest of Ireland in May 1650, and in the following month undertook the preventive campaign against Scotland, Fairfax having resigned as commander-in-chief because he thought the Scots should not be compelled to war. Cromwell entered Scotland on 22 July 1650; the poem, presumably, was written between his return from Ireland and that date.

Though the tone and some of the details derive from Horace, as the title suggests, Marvell also remembered and imitated what Lucan had written, in his epic *Pharsalia*, about Julius Caesar and Pompey. On the Horatian antecedents see John Coolidge, 'Marvell and Horace', *Modern Philology*, 43 (1965), 111-20. Annabel Patterson takes the mode of the poem to be that of 'conditional praise' (61). A strong and direct indebtedness to *Il Principe* is demonstrated by Brian Vickers, 'Machiavelli and Marvell's "Horatian Ode"', *Notes and Queries* (March 1989), 32–8.

The historical circumstances of the moment are fully described by Blair Worden, *The Historical Journal*, 27 (1984), 525–47; and see also Michael Wilding, *Dragons Teeth*, ch. 5.

l. 2. *now:* 'in times like these'. The opening lines (1–8) are adapted from Lucan, *Pharsalia*, i. 239–43.

l. 9. *restless:* a trait of Lucan's Caesar. The passage ll. 9–24 imitates *Pharsalia*, i. 143–55.   *cease:* rest.

80 l. 15. *thorough:* (Bodleian MS); through (*1681* has 'through').
side: (1) party; (2) the lightning is conceived as tearing through the side of its own body the cloud.

ll. 19–20. *And with . . . oppose:* to pen him in will produce an even more violent reaction than to fight against him.

l. 20. *more:* worse; a Latinism; cf. *Pharsalia.* l. 1: *'Bella . . . plus quam civilia'* (Craze).

l. 23. *Caesar:* Charles I, beheaded in 1649.

l. 24. *laurels:* thought to be proof against lightning and worn by Roman emperors.

l. 32. *bergamot:* a variety of pear.

l. 35. *kingdom: 1681;* 'kingdoms' Bodleian MS, Thompson.

l. 38. *ancient rights:* see 'Tom May's Death', l. 69.

l. 42. *penetration:* see note on 'Flecknoe', l. 99.

l. 46. *Where his . . . scars:* i.e. the scars he gave.

ll. 47–52. *And . . . case:* In 1648 the king, noting the increased hostility of the Army Council, took flight from his palace at Hampton Court to Carisbrooke on the Isle of Wight. He did not receive the expected welcome; the governor treated him as a prisoner. Thus his flight was in part responsible for what happened later, but the contemporary rumour that Cromwell engineered it—which is what Marvell here has in mind—appears to be without foundation.

l. 49. *subtile:* finely woven.

81 l. 52. *case:* cage.

l. 53. *actor:* this theatrical figure is sustained in l. 54 ('tragic scaffold'—stages for the acting of tragedies), l. 56 (clapping), and l. 58 (scene). John Carswell (*TLS*, 1 Aug. 1952, 501) suggests that ll. 57–64 constitute a faintly ironic criticism of an actor's performance. One contemporary account of the king's trial was called *Tragicum Theatrum Actorum.* The fact that the execution took place on a scaffold outside the Banqueting House (in which Charles had formerly acted in masques) gives additional force to the figure.

l. 56. *clap:* some said that the soldiers around the scaffold were ordered to clap, with the object of rendering the king's words inaudible.

l. 59. *keener:* keener than the axe's edge. The Latin *acies* means both 'eyesight' and 'blade'. 'It is recorded by one [eye-witness] that he had never seen the king's eyes brighter than in his last moment, and by another he more than once inquired about the sharpness of the axe' (C. V. Wedgwood, *Poetry and Politics under the Stuarts* (1961), 101-2).

l. 60. *try:* test.

ll. 63-4. *But bowed . . . bed:* 'The Venetian ambassador reported that the executioners had prepared for resistance on the part of the king by arranging to drag his head down by force; but he told them this was unnecessary, and voluntarily placed his head on the block' (Christopher Hill, *Puritanism and Revolution* (1958), 360 n.).

l. 66. *forced:* two syllables; gained by force.

ll. 67-72. *So . . . fate:* the story is told by Pliny, *Natural History*, xxviii. 4. The excavator of the foundations of the temple of Jupiter Capitolium found 'a man's head, face and all, whole and sound: which sight . . . plainly foretold that [Rome] should be chief castle of the empire and the capital place of the whole world' (Livy, *Annals*, i. 55.6, tr. Philemon Holland) (Donno). Hodge remarks that in Livy's version of the story the head is discovered by Tarquin, later banished as a tyrant (126).

l. 74. *in one year:* Cromwell's Irish campaign lasted from August 1649 to May 1650.

l. 76. *act and know:* this commends Cromwell for contemplative and active virtue, resuming the theme of ll. 29-37.

ll. 77-90. *They . . . skirts:* reminiscent of Lucan, ix. 192-200 (magnanimity of Pompey).

l. 77. *They:* the Irish. Irish testimony would be hard to find at the time (or, one might add, later).

l. 81. *yet:* either 'nevertheless' or 'up to now'.

l. 82. *still:* either 'always' or 'up to now'.

ll. 85. *Commons':* Bodleian MS, Thompson; 'Common' *1681*.

l. 87. *what he may:* so far as he can.

82 l. 95. *lure:* a lure was made of feathers. During training the hawk could expect to find food in it, and on active service return to it when the falconer calls.

l. 100. *crown: 1681*; 'crowns' Bodleian MS, Thompson.

l. 104. *climacteric:* Critical, marking an epoch (stressed on the first and third syllables).

l. 105. *Pict:* the name of a Celtic tribe inhabiting Scotland; chosen rather than 'Scot' for the sake of the pun in the next line.

l. 106. *parti-coloured:* variously coloured (Latin *pingere, pictum*, to paint). The Scots were generally regarded as fickle and treacherous. (There is also a pun on 'party'.)

l. 107. *sad:* severe, or steadfast.

l. 110. *mistake:* because of his coloured camouflage.

l. 116. *thy: 1681*; 'the' Thompson.

ll. 117–18. *Besides . . . night:* usually interpreted as referring to the cross-hilt of the sword, but this would imply that the sword is held hilt upmost, and this sword is 'erect'. Its power against the forces of darkness may then derive, as John M. Wallace suggests, from 'a sun-like glitter on the blade' (*PMLA* 77, 1961, 44). Elsie Duncan-Jones explains the lines as alluding to the pagan belief (Odyssey, ix. 48, *Aeneid*, vi. 260) that spirits of the underworld fear cold iron.

ll. 119–20. *The same arts . . . maintain:* a commonplace of political theory; for references see John M. Wallace, 43 and notes, 48–54.

Tom May's Death. Thomas May (1599–1650), historian, court poet, and translator of Lucan in a version known to Marvell, had been close to Ben Jonson, who wrote commendatory verse for the Lucan translation. He transferred his allegiance to the Parliamentary cause during the Civil War and wrote a history of the Long Parliament. This attack on May, presumably written soon after May's death on 13 November 1650, and so quite soon after the Horatian Ode, has been a puzzle to commentators, not made easier by the use of the expression 'ancient rights' (l. 69), since those rights were what Charles I had pleaded for in vain, not only in the poem but at his trial; for he asked how any citizen could call his life and possessions his own 'if power without right daily make new, and abrogate the fundamental laws of the land' (quoted in *The Letters and Speeches of Oliver Cromwell*, ed. W. C. Abbott (1937), i. 738). No entirely convincing solution has been offered. See, for example, Warren Chernaik, *The Poet's Time* (1983), 174 ff. ('far from being incompatible, [the two poems] are in many ways companion pieces'; the disapproval of rebellion in the poem 'need not be taken as reflecting the poet's persuasion'). Gerard Reedy in '"An Horatian Ode" and "Tom May's Death"', *Studies in English Literature*, 20 (1980), argues that Marvell's quarrel was based on disagreements between rival positions on the Parliamentary side, and Marvell may have disliked Tom May for his venality or for some personal reason. Christopher Hill (in Patrides, ed.) suggests that the poem was revised after the Restoration, when May's body was exhumed from Westminster Abbey in 1661, ll. 85–90 being a comment on this event.

'Tom May's Death' was omitted from the Bodleian MS. The fact has led some to question its authenticity.

l. 1. *drunk:* May died in his sleep, according to Aubrey, 'after drinking with his chin tied with his cap (being fat); suffocated'.

l. 6. *Stephen's Alley:* May lived here in Westminster. It was a well-known street of many taverns.   *grass?* Cooke; 'grass' *1681.*

l. 7. *The Pope's Head . . . Mitre:* common inn signs.

l. 8. *still:* always.

83   l. 10. *Ares:* perhaps an innkeeper.

l. 13. *Ben:* Ben Jonson, famous for his 'mountain belly'. He contributed laudatory verse to May's translation of Lucan's *Pharsalia.*

l. 18. *Brutus and Cassius:* heroes to republicans, but the darkest villains to royalists or imperialists. Dante places them with Judas in the mouths of Satan (*Inferno*, xxiv. 64–9).

l. 21. *Emanthian:* Cooke; 'Emilthian' *1681.*

ll. 21–4. *'Cups . . . health':* a parody of the opening lines of May's translation of Lucan:

> Wars more than civil on Emathian plains
> We sing; rage licensed; where great Rome distains
> In her own bowels her victorious swords . . .

l. 26. *translated:* by death and by Jonson.

l. 27. *stumbling:* May is said to have had a stammer, but of course he is here represented as drunk.

l. 29. *friend:* Jonson had addressed May as his 'chosen friend' in *Underwoods,* 21.

l. 38. *Like Pembroke . . . masque:* Lord Pembroke, the Lord Chamberlain, broke his staff on May at a court masque in 1634, 'not knowing who he was'. May was compensated.

l. 41. *Polydore . . . Goth:* Polydore Vergil, an Italian historian who came to the English court early in the sixteenth century and wrote a flattering *Historia Anglia* for Henry VII; and three barbarian tribes.

ll. 44–8. *On them . . . Cicero:* May was fond of making parallels between Parliamentary and Roman history.

84   l. 50. *As Bethlem's . . . Loreto walk:* the house of the Virgin was said to have been miraculously transported to Loreto (from Nazareth, not from Bethlehem).

l. 54. *Those . . . May:* May wrote a *Continuation of Lucan's Historical Poem till the death of Julius Caesar.*

l. 57. *more worthy:* Sir William Davenant became Poet Laureate in 1637, when May thought he would be appointed.

l. 60. *gazette-writer:* hack journalist ('gazette' stressed on the first syllable).

l. 62. *basket:* The *borsa* in which the warring Florentine sects of Guelphs and Ghibellines cast their votes.

l. 68. *world's:* Cooke; 'world' *1681*.

l. 69. *ancient rights:* see 'Horatian Ode', l. 38 (p. 83).

l. 74. *chronicler to Spartacus:* historian of the revolutionary Parliament. Spartacus was the leader of the slaves' revolt against Rome in 73–71 BC.

l. 75. *equal:* just.

l. 82. *Who thy . . . pay:* the Council of State voted £100 for May's burial in Westminster Abbey.

l. 88. *As th' eagle's . . . divide:* eagle feathers were supposed to rot those of other birds.

l. 90. *Phlegethon:* a river of Hades.

85 l. 91. *Cerebus:* three-headed watchdog of Hades.

l. 92. *Megaera:* serpent-haired Fury.

l. 93. *Ixion's wheel:* one of the torments of Hades.

l. 94. *the perpetual vulture feel:* like Prometheus.

To his worthy Friend Doctor Witty upon his Translation of the 'Popular Errors'. Robert Witty was a schoolmaster and later a physician in Hull. He translated a Latin work by James Primrose, another Hull doctor, on common errors and myths about medicine. Witty's translation was published in 1651 and Marvell's commendatory verses were printed therein. They were republished in 1681. Our text is mainly from *1681*, which does not differ in substance from *1651*.

l. 4. *cypress:* of fine linen.

ll. 4–16. *Take . . . spots:* Margoliouth notices these lines as 'one of the few scraps of Marvell's literary criticism'.

l. 17. *Celia:* perhaps Mary Fairfax; see 'Upon Appleton House', ll. 707–8 (p. 73). Marvell may have written these lines at Nun Appleton in the winter of 1650/1.

86 l. 30. *caudles:* gruels.   *almond-milk:* preparation of blanched almonds and water, used as an emollient.

The Character of Holland. The first hundred lines, together with an eight-line conclusion not by Marvell, were published in 1665. The whole work appeared in *1681*. Marvell probably wrote it in 1653, after the English victory over the Dutch fleet off Portugal in February, and before the engagement of 3 June, in which Deane was killed.

l. 5. *alluvion:* matter deposited by flood or inundation.

l. 18. *Thorough:* through.

ll. 19–20. *And . . . ground:* the figure is from bear-baiting.

87 l. 24. *leap-frog:* 'Frogs' was an occasional nickname for the Dutch.

l. 26. *Mare Liberum:* the title of a book by the Dutch lawyer and scholar Grotius claiming the freedom of the seas. The Commonwealth government claimed the Channel as English and required foreign ships to salute the English flag.

l. 28. *level-coil:* a rough game, one player unseating the other (*lever le cul*).

l. 32. *cabillau:* codfish.

l. 34. *Heeren:* gentlemen.

l. 36. *duck and drake:* skimming flat stones across water.

l. 45. *Leak:* leaky.

l. 49. *dyke-grave:* officer in charge of sea-walls.

l. 53. *Half-anders:* literally, 'half-different'. Here, not Hollanders (Whole-anders).

l. 62. *Poor-John:* dried hake.

88 l. 65. *Margaret:* a legendary Dutch countess who had 365 children at a birth.

l. 66. Hans-in-Kelder. A child in the womb.   *Hans-town:* a member of the Hanseatic league of cities.

l. 78. *village:* The Hague, which was denied the status of a town till the Napoleonic wars.

l. 80. Hogs: *Hoog-mogenden* ('high and mighty') was the style in which the States-General were addressed.   *Bores:* Boors (with a pun on 'boars' and 'Boers').

l. 82. *Civilis:* the chief of the Batavi in the fight against Rome, AD 69.

89 l. 86. *chafing-dish:* the Dutch carried stoves to church.

l. 88. *a wooden:* 1665; 'wooden' *1681*.

l. 90. *western end:* buttocks.

l. 94. *butter-coloss:* butter-box (nickname for Dutchman).

l. 95. *towns of Beer:* place-names beginning with Beer- or Bier-.

l. 96. *snick and sneer:* cut and thrust.

l. 98. *Cut . . . to a man:* Deinocrates the sculptor wanted to cut Mount Athos into the shape of Alexander. They want to cut each other's formless bulk into human shape.

l. 107. *vail:* salute by lowering colours; here, surrender.

l. 113. *Jus Belli et Pacis:* Grotius wrote *De Jure Belli et Pacis* (*On the Law of War and Peace*), 1625.

l. 114. *burgomaster of the sea:* Admiral Van Tromp.

l. 115. *gun power:* fortified spirits.   *brand wine:* Brandy.

l. 116. *linstock:* forked staff holding a lighted match.

l. 118. *sore:* Gen. 34: 25.

l. 120. *case-butter:* Cannister shot using butter (i.e. in this instance consisting of nothing more dangerous than butter).   *bullet-cheese:* bullets made of cheese.

l. 123. *kindly:* according to her nature.

l. 124. *A wholesome danger . . . ports:* Blake took refuge in port after an engagement with Van Tromp in November 1652.

l. 127. *careen:* be heeled over on their sides for repair.

l. 130. *halcyon:* see 'Appleton House', l. 669, and 'The Gallery', l. 135. The halcyon was sometimes said to nest during a period of calm at the winter solstice.

l. 134. *corruptible:* accented on the third syllable. Several officers were discharged after an inquiry into the action of November 1652.

l. 135. *Bucentore:* the Doge's galley, centre of the ceremony of Venice wedding the sea.

l. 137. *now:* Bodleian MS; 'how' *1681.*   *the: 1681* (most copies); 'their' Bodleian MS, *1681* (Huntington copy).   *seven provinces:* The United Provinces of the Netherlands.

l. 138. *our infant Hercules:* the original Hercules strangled serpents as a baby; but ours—the new Commonwealth—was like the mature hero, for he strangled the Hydra.

l. 139. *wants:* we have chopped it off (unlike the Hydra, the Dutch have only one neck).

ll. 141–4. *Or . . . refuse:* 'Unless, if the Dutch sued for peace, our rulers declined the approach lest the English youth lost the habit of war.' (The difficulty arises from the parenthesis; either, though the youth would surely not do so, or surely the government wouldn't behave so.)

90 l. 150. *Deane, Monck, and Blake:* Deane and Monck were colonels, appointed generals of the fleet in association with Blake. Deane was killed 3 June 1653.

The First Anniversary of the Government under His Highness the Lord Protector. Published as an anonymous quarto in 1655 in an edition apparently authorized by the Parliamentary government, and reprinted, but cancelled, in most copies of *1681* except the British Library's and the Huntington's.

Cromwell became Protector in December 1653. When Marvell wrote the poem he was at Eton, tutor to Cromwell's protégé William Dutton.

J. A. Mazzeo has argued that Marvell represents Cromwell here as a Davidic king; the concept of the *regnum Davidicum* had long been associated with European kingship, for example in coronation rituals (*Reason and the Imagination: Studies in the history of ideas 1660–1800*, ed. J. A. Mazzeo, 1962). John M. Wallace treats the poem as a 'deliberative' one, about Cromwell instituting a new dynasty, Marvell holding that the choice of king was human, but that anointment ought to follow; after election, the grace of God. The succession must be assured against accidents and Fifth Monarchy machinations (*Destiny his Choice*, 1968). See also, on the politics of the poem, Steven Zwicker, 'Models of Governance in Marvell's "The First Anniversary"', *Criticism*, 16 (1974), 1–12 (Marvell is one who rejects the idea of Cromwell as king, but regards him as a divine instrument sent to heal England, herald of a millennium when Christ will rule). Also, on the chiliastic element, see Stocker, 13–27, Chernaik, 43–59 and 68 ff.

The poem has seven principal sections: (1) 1–48, a celebration of Cromwell's monarchic vigour and integrity; (2) 49–116, his building of a harmonious state; (3) 117–58, delay in arriving of the millennium because of human folly; (4) 159–220, Cromwell's coach accident in Hyde Park, September 1654; (5) 221–92, defence of Cromwell against the charge that he exercised arbitrary power; (6) 293–324, attack on the Fifth Monarchy men; (7) 325–402, envy and admiration of foreign princes, and conclusion.

Title: *1655*, Bodleian MS; 'The First Anniversary of the Government under O.C.' *1681*. (*1681*'s title is presumably a censored version.)

l. 1. *curlings*: undulations.

l. 12. *And shines the jewel . . . ring*: like the sun in the zodiac.

ll. 13–14. *'Tis he the force . . . acts*: compare the different version in the 'Horatian Ode', ll. 34–6.

l. 16. *Saturn*: which had the longest orbit of the known planets.

l. 17. *Platonic years*: a Platonic year is the period required for all the planets to return to their original relative positions; estimated at 36,000 years.

l. 20. *China clay*: it was believed that the Chinese made porcelain by burying clay in the ground.

l. 23. *some*: some king.

ll. 24–6. *Took in by proxy . . . lost*: various more or less contemporary instances of this not unusual practice of delegating the fighting and taking the credit have been adduced. There is an early example in 2 Samuel 11, where David leaves the work to Joab while he stays at home and seduces Bathsheba; in chapter 12 he takes the credit.

91 l. 27. *wrong*: a verb.

l. 30. *common enemy*: the subjects.

l. 33. *temple:* David was commanded to leave the building of the Temple to Solomon (1 Chron. 28).

l. 36. *perfect:* stressed on the first syllable.

l. 41. *image-like:* like clock-figures striking the hour on a bell.

ll. 47–8. *Learning . . . sphere:* a reference to a familiar body of ideas about *musica humana* and its relation to the harmony of the spheres (see, for full treatment, J. Hollander, *The Untuning of the Sky*, 1961).

l. 49. *Amphion:* He built the wall at Thebes by making stones move to music; a stock figure in the formal *laudes musicae*.

l. 50. *the god:* Hermes.

l. 60. *joining: 1655*: 'joyng' *1681*.

l. 66. *seven:* Appropriately, since there were 'six notes of music' and the seventh provided what we would call an octave.

92 l. 68. *Instrument:* A pun; Cromwell's Protectorate was instituted by an Instrument of Government in 1653.

l. 69. *hack:* (1) muddle; (2) to break a note in music.

ll. 69–70 *While tedious statesmen . . . back:* earlier attempts to frame a new constitution had succeeded only in reducing liberty.

l. 81. *bends:* consents.

l. 85. *attractive:* in the literal sense: he draws them as Amphion did the stones.

l. 90. *contignation:* a joining together of boards.

l. 95. *opposed:* three syllables.

l. 99. *a place:* Archimedes said that given a fulcrum he could move the earth.

l. 101. *aspects:* an astrological term. Planets in varying positions have good or ill aspects towards the earth.

l. 104. *influence:* also astrological.

ll. 105–8. *O would they rather . . . lead*: Ps 2: 10–12.

93 l. 110. *latter days:* Dan. 2: 28, 10: 14. These are apocalyptic lines.

Many believed in the approaching Fifth Monarchy of the Saints (Dan. 7: 18), after the destruction of the Great Whore (Rome) (Rev. 17: 5) and the Beast (Rev. 17: 3).

l. 115. *Indians:* as one of the nations, they should be brought in, not subdued.

l. 116. *Jew:* the Conversion of the Jews would precede the Latter Days. Cromwell, in 1656, allowed the readmission of the Jews to England, expressly to facilitate this development.

l. 123. *prevents the east:* anticipates the dawn.

l. 125. *hollo:* huntsman's cry.

l. 128. *thorough:* through.

l. 140. *latest day:* Day of Judgement.

94 ll. 151–2. *And stars . . . flail:* Rev. 12: 3–4, and Milton's 'Ode on the Morning of Christ's Nativity', ll. 168–72.

l. 152. *volumes:* coils.

l. 153. *suspend:* at the Flood.

l. 157. *landing nature:* about to reach port; cf. 'A Dialogue between the Soul and Body', ll. 29–30.

l. 161. *saint-like mother:* Elizabeth Cromwell died 16 Nov. 1654, aged 93.

ll. 171–2. *Thy breast . . . prophecies:* alluding to various plots against Cromwell by Levellers and Fifth Monarchists, some gaining the impetus from interpretations of biblical prophecies.

l. 175. *How near:* by what a narrow margin.

ll. 177–8. *Our brutish fury . . . hurried thee:* on 29 Sept. 1654, Cromwell's coach, drawn by six horses, overturned in Hyde Park.

l. 182. *yearly.* celebrating the events of the year.

l. 184. *purling:* embroidery.

95 l. 197. *Nor through . . . wanton air:* cf. Virgil, *Georgics,* i. 375–6.

l. 203. *panic:* Marvell derives from the Greek for 'all' (*pan*).

ll. 205–6. *centre:* cf. 'Resolved Soul', l. 71, and ll. 363–4 below.
sphere: The fourth sphere of the pre-Copernican astronomy was the sun's.

ll. 215–20. *But thee . . . mantle rent:* cf. 2 Kgs. 2: 11–13, and Plato, *Republic,* viii. 566.

ll. 221–32. *For all delight . . . body strong:* cf. 'Horatian Ode', ll. 27–32.

96 ll. 233–8. *Till at the seventh time . . . kings:* cf. 1 Kgs. 18: 44–6.

l. 238. *though forewarned:* this refers to the king.

l. 239. *since:* since 1649.

ll. 249–56. *When Gideon . . . son:* Judg. 8: 1–23. Cromwell's achievements are aligned with Gideon's.

ll. 257–64. *Thou with . . . didst awe:* Judg. 9: 7–15, a parable about the olive, the fig, the vine, and the bramble, which accepts the crown the others refuse; Jotham gives it a political application.

l. 262. *Had quickly levelled . . . top:* an allusion to the Levellers.

ll. 265–78. *So have I seen . . . prevent:* the ship of state was safer in the open sea—the plots and plans of various parties being represented as the rocks and shallows some mistook for land.

l. 269. *Tritons:* sea gods.

l. 270. *corposants:* balls of fire seen on the masts and rigging of ships.

97 l. 281. *bounders:* limits.

ll. 293–310. *Yet such a . . . Alcoraned:* referring to the many religious sects of the times, especially the Fifth Monarchy Men (l. 297).

l. 293. *Chammish:* like Ham (Vulgate, Cham), Gen. 9: 24–5.

l. 300. *Might muster . . . ten:* i.e. if one heresy equalled ten men.

ll. 301–2. *What thy misfortune . . . fall:* 'spirit' alludes to the cant of the sects; those possessed by it behave like epileptics (l. 302).

l. 303. *Mahomet:* his revelation was supposedly accompanied by something like an epileptic fit.

l. 305. *Feake and Simpson:* Christopher Feake and John Simpson, imprisoned in 1654 for preaching against Cromwell.

l. 307. *rant:* alluding to the sect of Ranters, fanatically antinomian.

l. 308. *tulipant:* turban.

l. 310. Alcoraned: turned into a holy book like the Koran.

l. 311. *locusts:* Rev. 9: 1–11; a passage generally associated with heretics.

l. 313. *Munser's rest:* Munster, in Westphalia, was taken in 1534 by the Anabaptists. This means: Anabaptists, etc., left over from Munster. Or possibly the reference is to Thomas Munzer, founder of the sect— 'Munzer's leavings'.

98 l. 315. *deface:* here with the sense 'efface'. They condemned the use of Scripture, having the Holy Spirit within them, and called all laws oppressive; thus these libertarians treated the Bible and law with the same contempt that they showed to personal adornment.

l. 319. *act the Adam and Eve:* Adamite sects went naked.

ll. 325–42. *So when . . . side:* this tale was first mentioned, mockingly, in Lucretius, *De Rerum Natura*, v. 973–6. It was again mentioned by

Manilius, *Astronomica*, i. 66–70, and Statius, *Thebaid*, iv. 282–4. The most obvious resemblance in Marvell's poem is to the lines of Statius (Duncan-Jones). This ancient tale presumably refers here to Cromwell's accident; he was at first reported dead.

l. 350. *both wars:* the Civil War and the Dutch War.

l. 352. *their:* conjectured by Margoliouth; 'our' *1655, 1681.*

99 l. 356. *shedding leaves:* a kind of goose was thought to be bred from leaves fallen into water.

l. 362. *brazen hurricanes:* bronze cannon.

l. 363. *That through . . . side:* cf. l. 205.

l. 366. *leaguers:* besieging forces.

l. 381. *enchased:* worked in together.

l. 384. *our knots:* alluding to the Gordian knot: whoever untied it would be master of the world. Alexander cut it.

100 ll. 401–2. *And as the angel . . . heal:* in John 5:4 an angel troubles the water and it cures the sick. Cromwell did the same by accepting the Protectorate in December 1653, and was about to do it again by dissolving Parliament in January 1655.

On the Victory obtained by Blake over the Spaniards. Presumably written June–early August 1657. News of Blake's victory reached England in late May; Blake died in early August. Sir Robert Blake (1599–1657) was one of Cromwell's admirals, a brilliant and aggressive commander. At the time of this action against Spanish treasure ships his health was much enfeebled by a wound received in an earlier battle.

The poem was first published anonymously in *A New Collection of Poems and Songs* (1674). In this version the allusions to Cromwell, to whom the poem is implicitly addressed, are excised, and there are other omissions. Our text is from *1681.* The poem is not in the Bodleian MS.

Title: 1681; 'On the victory over the Spaniards in the Bay of Santa Cruz, in the Island of Tenerife.' *1674.*

l. 4. *guilt:* with pun on 'gilt'.

l. 20. *streamers:* pennons.

l. 25. *One of which:* Tenerife, with its tall peak.

101 l. 28. *Trees . . . supply:* the idea may be that dew descending from the trees on the top does the office of rain.

l. 39. *Your:* i.e. Cromwell's.

l. 40. *kings:* notable because Marvell had thought it right for Cromwell to refuse the crown. This lends some force to Lord's rejection of the poem. (It is not in the Bodleian MS.)

l. 46. *this one peace:* England and Spain had been at peace since 1630.

l. 54. *the fancied drink:* nectar.

l. 66. *your present:* your present conquests.

102 l. 91. *sources:* small forts.

103 l. 117. *Stayner:* Sir Richard Stayner, one of Blake's captains.

l. 118. *To give him laurel . . . plate:* this victory gained him honours (he was knighted for his deed) as the last (he intercepted a Spanish treasure fleet) gave him prize money.

l. 132. *its:* the fire's.

l. 139. *or . . . or:* either . . . or.

104 *Two Songs at the Marriage of the Lord Fauconberg and the Lady Mary Cromwell.* Mary Cromwell, third daughter of the Protector, married Lord Fauconberg on 19 Nov. 1657. These songs probably belong to a musical entertainment devised for the wedding.

l. 1. *eyes:* as well as his stars.

105 l. 27. *thorough:* through.

l. 30. *Anchises:* lover of Venus, but here Robert Rich, who a week earlier had married Cromwell's fourth daughter, Frances.

l. 35. *Latmos' top:* the place where Cynthia wooed Endymion.

106 *Second song*

l. 3. *northern shepherd's:* Fauconberg was from Yorkshire and a kinsman of Fairfax.

l. 4. *Menalca's daughter:* Menalca is, like the other names here, familiar in pastoral poetry. In this case he is Cromwell.

107 l. 26. *silly:* innocent.

108 l. 34. *Marina's:* Marina is another pastoral name, like Damon: perhaps arbitrarily chosen, it seems to have no marine connotation.

l. 43. *beauty's hire:* obscure: presumably her beauty is the reward of his virtue?

A Poem upon the Death of his late Highness the Lord Protector. Together with the 'Horatian Ode' and 'The First Anniversary', this poem was cancelled from *1681*, though not from the British Library's copy. However, even in that copy 140 lines are wanting (185–324). These were provided by Thompson, but occur also in the Bodleian MS, which is probably the book Thompson describes as having come into his hands when he had finished preparing his edition.

Cromwell died on 3 Sept 1658. Marvell's poem is a long funeral elegy on the general pattern of such things (see Wallerstein, *Seventeenth-*

Century Poetic, 1950), but it also reveals some of the political tensions experienced by the poet at this time.

Text: ll. 1–184 from *1681*; ll. 185–324 from Bodleian MS.

title: Bodleian MS; 'A Poem upon the Death of O.C.' *1681*.

l. 2. *every hair:* Matt. 10:30.

l. 4. *seen the period:* foreseen the completion.

l. 14. *or clemency that would: His* clemency was such that no one wanted to hurt him. (?)

109 l. 16. *angry heaven:* cf. 'Horatian Ode', l. 26.

l. 21. *signed:* assigned.

l. 22. *Those nobler weaknesses . . . mind:* cf. Milton's 'Lycidas', l. 71, and 'Flecknoe', ll. 27–8. *mind: 1681*; 'kind' Thompson, Bodleian MS.

l. 30. *Eliza:* Cromwell's second daughter Eliza died on 6 Aug. 1658.

ll. 39–40. *When with . . . fairer mind:* cf. Donne, 'The Second Anniversary', ll. 244–5, and 'A Funeral Elegy' (following 'The First Anniversary'), ll. 59–61.

l. 45. *not knowing:* i.e. not by knowing.

l. 54. *And him . . . racks:* The father having within him the image of the daughter must suffer the pain of her fever (the image compared to a wax doll melting in the heat).

110 l. 62. *feigns:* dissimulates.

ll. 67–8. *And now . . . had word:* alluding to Ovid's story of Scylla, who cut off from her father's head the purple lock on which his life depended.

l. 87. *immortal tried:* tested in other ways, he proved immortal.

111 l. 108. *celebrates:* Bodleian MS, Margoliouth; 'celebrate' *1681*.

l. 113. *First the great thunder . . . sent:* there was a great storm on 2 Sept.

l. 121. *lead:* Grosart, Margoliouth; 'dead' *1681*, Bodleian MS.

l. 128. *not to see:* in order not to see. There had been an epidemic of fever earlier in the year.

l. 131. *air:* i.e. one of the elements.

l. 137. *The stars . . . power:* Judg. 5: 20: 'They fought from heaven; the stars in their course fought against Sisera.'

112 l. 139. *cast:* calculate (as in astronomy).

l. 144. *Twice:* at Dunbar, 3 Sept. 1650, and at Worcester, 3 Sept. 1651.

l. 146. *He marched . . . ending war:* at the battle of Worcester, Cromwell bridged the Severn and fell on the flank of the Scots.

l. 154. *Gave chase . . . coast:* In Sept. 1658 a Spanish force under the Prince de Ligne was defeated in Flanders by a French army with an English contingent.

l. 162. *Than those of Moses . . . eyes:* Deut. 34: 6.

ll. 173–4. *Who planted . . . Indian ore.* The capture of Dunkirk from the Spaniards (1658), and of Jamaica (1655).

l. 176. *worthies:* King Arthur was made one of the nine worthies.

l. 178. *Confessor:* Edward.

113 l. 180. *manned:* 'made a man of'.

l. 181. *inward mail:* Eph. 6:11.

l. 187. *Preston's field:* Cromwell defeated the Scots under Hamilton near Preston, in August 1648.

l. 188. *impregnable Clonmel:* Clonmel was attacked unsuccessfully by Cromwell, but the Irish subsequently evacuated it (May 1650). This was the last incident in Cromwell's Irish campaign.

l. 180. *And where . . . Fenwick scaled:* at the battle of the Dunes in June 1658, which preceeded the occupation of Dunkirk, Lt.-Col. Roger Fenwick was mortally wounded in storming a sandhill. The day was a day of public prayer.

l. 190. *The sea between:* although the sea was between.

ll. 191–2. *What man . . . Gibeon stayed:* Josh. 10: 12–14: 'And there was no day like that before it or after it, that the Lord harkened unto the voice of a man' (v. 14).

l. 194. *He conquered God . . . men:* See Gen. 32: 24–9.

ll. 201–2. *Friendship . . . name:* the Protector's branch of the Cromwell family was founded by his great-grandfather Richard Williams, nephew on his mother's side of Thomas Cromwell, Earl of Essex. His friendship with his uncle resulted in his being knighted and in his adoption of the surname Cromwell.

l. 203. *But within . . . all:* but while friendship attaches to one object, Cromwell's tenderness extended unto all.

l. 215. *cast:* calculated; cf. l. 139; or perhaps 'diagnosed'.

114 l. 234. *Janus' double gate:* The *ianus geminus* in the Forum at Rome.

l. 242. *David:* 'And David danced before the Lord with all his might' (2 Sam. 6: 14).

l. 245. *Francisca:* Cromwell's youngest daughter, Frances.

l. 259. *feign:* Imagine.

115 ll. 264. *honoured wreaths:* oak garlands awarded for statesmanship.

ll. 269–70. *The tree . . . grew:* cf. 'Eyes and Tears', ll. 5–6; also ll. 273–4.

l. 275. *seat:* Bodleian MS; 'state' Thompson.

l. 276. *Seeing how little . . . great:* perhaps meaning: when they are high our eye diminishes their stature; it is when we see them at our own height that we understand their greatness.

l. 282. *Cynthia:* the moon.

l. 287. *pitch:* height (as used in falconry).

l. 291. *at:* conjectured by Margoliouth; 'yet' Bodleian MS.

116 l. 305. *Richard:* Richard Cromwell (1626–1712) was proclaimed Protector on the day of his father's death, but resigned the title in Apr. 1659.

l. 317. *enchased:* adorned.

On Mr Milton's 'Paradise Lost'. These verses, signed A.M., were prefixed to the second edition of *Paradise Lost* (1674) and reprinted in *1681*. Marvell is known to have supported Milton at the time of his greatest danger at the Restoration, and he also defended him in the second part of *The Rehearsal Transprosed* (1673).
    Text from *1681*.

117 ll. 18–22. *Jealous I was . . . play:* Dryden asked and got Milton's permission to adapt *Paradise Lost* for the stage. The result was an 'opera' in rhymed couplets, called *The State of Innocence*, published in 1677, and probably never performed. Marvell obviously disliked Dryden, partly no doubt because he changed sides at the Restoration, and Dryden retaliated in the preface to *Religio Laici*.

l. 25. *that:* Bodleian MS; 'and' *1681*, Margoliouth.

l. 30. *detect:* expose.

l. 33. *treat'st: 1674*; 'treats' *1681*.

l. 39. *The bird . . . paradise.* The bird of paradise was supposed to have no feet and to remain in perpetual flight.

l. 43. *Tiresias:* the blind prophet of Thebes.

l. 45. *mightst: 1674*, Bodleian MS; 'might' *1681*.

l. 46. *rhyme:* see Milton's adverse comments on rhyme in the prefatory remarks to *Paradise Lost*. Dryden's *State of Innocence* is mostly in heroic couplets. Milton is said to have given Dryden permission to 'tag' his verses.

l. 47. *Town-Bays:* Buckingham's *Rehearsal (*1672) presented Dryden as Bays, and the nickname stuck. See *The Rehearsal Transprosed, passim.*

l. 49. *bushy points:* used for fastening hose; the ends were often tasselled. He means that whereas we use such frivolous ornaments only for 'fashion', such poets as Dryden employ them (viz., rhymes) as necessary to their halting verse.

ll. 51–2. *I too . . . commend:* caught up in this fashion, I can't use the word 'praise' but must say 'commend' for the sake of the rhyme.

l. 54. *In number . . . measure:* Wisd. 11: 20: 'thou hast ordered all things in measure and number and weight.'

Further Reading

(The place of publication is London unless otherwise specified.)

EDITIONS

The Complete Work in Verse and Prose of Alexander Marvell, ed. Alexander B. Grosart (4 vols., 1872–5).

The Poems and Letters of Andrew Marvell, ed. H. M. Margoliouth (2 vols., Oxford, 1927; 3rd edn. revised by Pierre Legouis and E. E. Duncan-Jones, 2 vols., Oxford, 1971).

The Selected Poems of Marvell, ed. Frank Kermode (New York, 1967).

Andrew Marvell: Complete Poetry, ed. George de F. Lord (New York, 1968; London, 1984).

Andrew Marvell, The Complete Poems, ed. Elizabeth Story Donno (1972).

Andrew Marvell: Selected Poetry and Prose, ed. Robert Wilcher (1986).

'The Rehearsal Transpros'd' and 'The Rehearsal Transpros'd: The Second Part', ed. D. I. B. Smith (Oxford, 1971).

BIOGRAPHIES

Kelliher, Hilton, *Andrew Marvell: Poet and Politician 1621–78* (1978).

Legouis, Pierre, *Andrew Marvell: Poet, Puritan, Patriot* (Oxford, 1965).

REFERENCE

Collins, Dan S., *Andrew Marvell: A Reference Guide* (Boston, Mass., 1981).

Guffey, George R., *A Concordance to the English Poems of Andrew Marvell* (Chapel Hill, NC, 1974).

CRITICAL

Bradbrook, M. C., and Lloyd Thomas, M. G., *Andrew Marvell* (Cambridge, 1940).

Brett, R. L. (ed.), *Andrew Marvell: Essays on the Tercentenary of his Death* (Oxford, 1979).

Carey, John (ed.), *Andrew Marvell: A Critical Anthology* (1969).

Chernaik, Warren L., *The Poet's Time: Politics and Religion in the Work of Andrew Marvell* (Cambridge, 1983).

Colie, Rosalie L., *'My Ecchoing Song': Andrew Marvell's Poetry of Criticism* (Princeton, NJ, 1970).

Craze, Michael, *The Life and Lyrics of Andrew Marvell* (1979).

Duncan-Jones, E. E., 'Marvell: A Great Master of Words', *Proceedings of the British Academy*, 61, *1975* (Oxford, 1976), pp. 267–90.

Eliot, T. S., 'Andrew Marvell', in *Selected Essays* (3rd edn., 1951).

Empson, William, *Some Versions of Pastoral* (1935).

Friedenreich, Kenneth, (ed.), *Tercentenary Essays in Honour of Andrew Marvell* (Hamden, Conn., 1977).

Friedman, Donald F., *Marvell's Pastoral Art* (1970).

Hodge, R. I. V., *Foreshortened Time: Andrew Marvell and Seventeenth Century Revolutions* (Cambridge, 1978).

Leishman, J. B., *The Art of Marvell's Poetry* (1966).

Lord, George de F. (ed.), *Andrew Marvell: A Collection of Critical Essays* (Englewood Cliffs, NJ, 1968).

Patrides, C.A. (ed.), *Approaches to Marvell: The York Tercentenary Essays* (1978).

Patterson, Annabel M., *Marvell and the Civic Crown* (Princeton, NJ, 1978).

Røstvig, Maren-Sofie, *The Happy Man: Studies in the Metamorphoses of a Classical Ideal* (Oslo, 1954).

Scoular, Kitty W., *Natural Magic: Studies in the Presentation of Nature in English Poetry from Spenser to Marvell* (Oxford, 1965).

Stocker, Margarita, *Apocalyptic Marvell: The Second Coming in Seventeenth Century Poetry* (Brighton, 1986).

Wallace, John M., *Destiny his Choice: The Loyalism of Andrew Marvell* (Cambridge, 1968).

Wilcher, Robert, *Andrew Marvell* (Cambridge, 1985).

Wilding, Michael, *Dragons Teeth: Literature in the English Revolution* (Oxford, 1987).

Index of First Lines